FOXHEAD BOOKS

TASTE

Daisy Rockwell

FOXHEAD BOOKS

© 2014 by Daisy Rockwell. All rights reserved.

Illustrations by Daisy Rockwell • Book design by Jenn Manley Lee

No part of this document may be reproduced or transmitted in any form or by any means, electronic, mechanical, photocopying, recording, or otherwise, without prior written permission of the author, with the exception of brief excerpts for inclusion in scholarly works or inclusion in reviews. For permissions or further information, post Potemkin Media Omnibus, Ltd. at 8 S. 3rd St., Tipp City, OH 45371

Rockwell, Daisy.
Taste / by Daisy Rockwell 210 p. 1.21cm.
1. Fiction. I. Taste.
ISBN-13 978-9-940876-04-3

For my mother

TASTE

Part 1 : Table

Fruit table (looking down)
From memory

1

"Here you will notice a very unusual piece," droned the docent. She waved her hand mechanically toward a low Victorian table of carved wood. I was stunned. Craning my neck to see over the shoulders of a family standing in front of me, I felt certain the table at which she gestured was in every way identical to a table my grandmother had once owned. As a young boy I had always loved that glass-topped table filled with waxen fruits. It had never crossed my mind that such a marvel could have a duplicate, but here it was, and in the home of the two men whom my grandfather had once claimed among his closest friends and associates.

"This table, a favorite of Louisa Schiffley's, would have accompanied her grandparents when they moved to Philadelphia from Hartford," the Schiffley House docent continued in her grating voice. "Louisa kept this table in her personal sitting room throughout her life, and on her death, willed it to her nephews with the property. This table is of rare and unusual design and we have been told that only two tables of this kind were shipped from the original manufacturer in London, England, in 1897."

My grandmother's table had been low and rectangular and made of highly polished wood, perhaps mahogany. The glass tabletop was a large display case for the colorful waxen fruits it contained. As a child, whenever I grew weary of the adults' conversations, I would gaze meditatively at the fruits, marveling at their elaborate design and effusive arrangement. It should be remarked that the table did not match the rest of the furnishings in the room, all of which were strictly in the modernist mold, forming bold geometric shapes and tinted in shades of mustard and white. It was natural, then, that it drew the eye, simply because it was much darker than anything else, except for a rather stern Victorian secretary standing stiffly against the wall just next to it.

After the death of my grandmother, family members asked if I, as her only grandson, would like anything from the house. Though I was still young, I immediately asked about the fruit table. No one seemed to remember it. When they looked into the matter, they learned that only a few items in the house had belonged to her personally, through family inheritance. In truth she had been my step grandmother, as my real grandmother had passed away many years before. Those few objects and pieces of furniture that were hers alone were to be distributed among a handful of nieces and nephews, perhaps the only legacy of any value she could actually will her own flesh and blood. To me this made the table all the more valuable, knowing that it had really been hers, not just something that went with the dominant décor. Everything else in that house had been so carefully tailored for its role as a stage set for a man of consequence.

The loss of a table I had never owned nor lived with did not strike me too hard at the time. I still had two keepsakes from Grand Jane, as I had called her: one was a small jewel-studded dagger with a brass handle encased in a leather sheath that she had once purchased in a bazaar in Morocco while traveling with my grandfather. Grand Jane used the dagger as a letter-opener, and knowing that I had admired it a great deal since early boyhood, she gave it to me as a gift on my twelfth birthday, when she thought I had attained sufficient maturity to handle the blade safely. The other keepsake was a first American edition of Dickens' *Our Mutual Friend* she had given me on the occasion of my graduation from secondary school, where I had shown promise in literary studies, her life's passion. I was in college when Grand Jane died, and had never really imagined that an object as substantial as the fruit table would make its way into my makeshift existence. Over time, my precise memory of it grew fainter, but the twinge of loss became subtly more palpable.

It was on that guided tour of the stately home Schiffley House that I first gazed upon that table that was to haunt me for so many days. The docent, a young graduate from one of the local colleges, had done her best to dismantle the impact of the combination of furnishings, pictures, wall and floor coverings, and light fixtures as they had been originally choreographed by the tastes and habits of their longtime owners. Excising each piece, one at a time, from the overall ensemble, she would remark on its age and provenance and the use to which it might have been put by various members of the Schiffley family, based on either research or conjecture, or a combination of the two.

"Notice the sewing table to your right. This table would have been used by the women in the family after dinner as they all gathered by the fire. The table itself is made of walnut, and dates to the 1850's. Hal Schiffley's wife, Tessa Schiffley, was known for her great fondness for textiles and sewing. According to her diary, this table was kept on the third floor, in the servants' quarters, at the time she moved into the house after her marriage to Hal Schiffley in 1955."

The singling out of the sewing table seemed to push back the shadows and shine a galling fluorescent light upon the narrow dark living room. Suddenly all the objects jumped back and lost the logic of their composition. I found myself imagining the docent as a light over an operating table, her words and explanations reducing the mysteries of life to a series of easily perceived tumors or polyps ready to be sliced out of the body of the room. Room after room was demystified for the bewildered tour group until we had climbed up and down the stairs of both the houses and passed through the series of three secret passageways between the two houses in the central, connective addition, or the Annex, as it was known.

Despite the clinical qualities of the tour, one was still

struck by the bizarreness of this last feature of Schiffley House. Where one would expect the architects to conceive of and build an addition with some usefulness in terms of living or work space, the Schiffleys had asked for no more than a connection, and one that was designed as a secret kept from the inside of the two halves of the house, while appearing perfectly obvious from the outside, since where before there had been no structure connecting the two houses, now there was one. On the inside of the houses, however, the passageways leading from one side to the other by way of the Annex were artfully disguised by trick doors set into the walls, complete with faux molding and *trompe l'oeil* paintings meant to deceive the innocent guest. On the other side of these trick doors, inside the Annex, were a series of small corridors, unadorned, barely lit, with no windows, carpets or pictures. It was almost as if the two brothers in their old age had become Siamese twins, reverting in some manner to a level of connection mirroring that which they might have experienced in the womb, had they been twins.

The tour was pleasant enough, but it was not until we reached the second floor of the second house, the house that had been occupied by Larry Schiffley, following the death of his aunt and benefactress, Louisa Schiffley, that my interest was piqued. We had entered the room that was said to have been Louisa Schiffley's personal sitting room, which had been kept more or less intact even after Larry Schiffley's family had moved in. It was a small room with pale green walls that seemed to encompass both the solitary melancholy of its chief inhabitant and designer, as well as her exquisite good taste. There were several fine prints on the walls, a minimal quantity of wooden furniture, and a short, overstuffed blue chintz sofa along the wall, which afforded a person seated there an unobstructed southern view of the city. The room also contained a low bookcase with some neatly bound volumes, a needlepoint stand, and a pianola on which the curators had placed some sheet music to indicate to the visitors Louisa Schiffley's fondness for music. Everything had been so nicely arranged, it had taken me a moment to recognize the truly extraordinary object in the room, the elegant fruit table in front of the sofa.

When I had returned from the tour of Schiffley House to my friend Lucinda's cubicle—she was newly hired as an assistant curator there—I was slightly dazed, but I did not tell her of the table. It seemed far too personal, the sort of emotional experience one does not easily express or articulate until much later. Why had it touched me so? I pondered this question as I stared out the window on my train journey home to Boston. A gray drizzle streaked aslant across the murky scratched windows. The familiar sights of New Jersey, and then New York and Connecticut, rushed by in a blur.

DAGGER
(Moroccan)

2

My visit to Schiffley House had been occasioned by an invitation to visit with Lucinda, an old college friend who had recently finished a certificate program in curating. Her excellent performance in the certificate program had helped her win a prestigious position at that stately home and archive in Philadelphia. The invitation came as a surprise, as I had not seen Lucinda in many years, though we had kept in touch and written letters occasionally. Perhaps she was lonely in Philadelphia, because she sent a paper invitation, written in a witty style on engraved heavy bond paper, with her monogram at the head. I was surprised that she would have commissioned such expensive and high quality paper for herself, considering that people rarely write letters these days, and that she usually refrained from making a show of her wealth. Later, when I had let slip a remark about the superb quality of the engraving, she had laughed with embarrassment and explained that it was a gift from an aunt with a tendency toward excessive tastes in stationary.

The invitation had been carefully penned in a flowery calligraphic style and included illustrations, small cartoon-like sketches she had drawn herself, of the kinds of sights we might see should I come to visit. On the agenda was a visit to the art museum, a stroll through the University campus with stops at various student cafés, a trip to see the Liberty Bell and a guided tour of the Betsy Ross House by a fellow curator friend. Of course, the main attraction was to be a personally guided tour through Schiffley House, including a visit to the Schiffley family archive. This last attraction persuaded me to buy a train ticket and make my way down to Philadelphia. The Schiffley family archive was not open to the public at that time and was said to contain many important documents regarding the history of the early development of the jet engine, including numerous documents pertaining to my research into my grandfather's work and historical legacy.

The Schiffley brothers, Hal and Larry, had been scions of an old New England family that moved down to Philadelphia in connection with railways, thus making their fortune anew. Two generations later, Hal and Larry Schiffley, influenced by the philosophical and political writings of my grandfather, had virtually bankrolled all research on the jet engine in the thirties on behalf of the United States government. The investment in the end trebled their family's assets and holdings through patent royalties and shares in the jet engine manufacturing industry, making them the third richest family in America in the forties and fifties.

Lucinda had some idea that I had been dabbling in research on my grandfather's associations with technology inventors with a view to writing a biography one day perhaps. The possibility of exploring the rarely seen correspondence between my grandfather and the Schiffley brothers was too much to pass up. These documents had been kept under lock and key by the archivists at Schiffley House for over a decade, even after they had been declassified by the government. After receiving Lucinda's generous invitation, I booked my ticket at once.

Lucinda had fixed Tuesday as the day we would visit Schiffley House, and had secured an appointment for me to speak with the head archivist about getting access to the Schiffley papers. This meant we would spend the weekend, and Monday, which was a holiday, engaged in the other sightseeing activities she had planned. Lucinda diligently checked off each item on the list of things she had promised we would do. On Tuesday we set out with great excitement for Schiffley House. It was another gray and wintry day and the breeze carried with it a damp chill that somehow managed to penetrate all sorts of foul-weather gear. My greatcoat, muffler and woolen hat felt thin and insubstantial as we walked briskly down the city streets.

Schiffley House does not look quite the same on such a day as it does in books. Such photographs are no doubt taken in midsummer when the lawns sloping up to the house are densely green, the trees are in full leaf, and the gray stone edifice of the twin adjoining houses that make up Schiffley House looks stern, even against a blue summer sky. On that January day, however, gray met gray, and looking up the slope of the lawn, crusted with ice and dirty snow, the eaves of the two halves of the house seemed two disapproving eyebrows glowering down at the shivering passersby who stumbled along the city street below.

As is fairly well known, the two houses were non-adjoining graystones built by Hal and Larry Schiffley's grandfather and his brother upon their arrival in Philadelphia. Hal and Larry had grown up in the house on the left. The house on the right had been occupied by their aged aunt Louisa Schiffley, a frugal woman who had never married and lived alone. At her death, it was discovered that she had made a vast fortune in a few wisely chosen investments. She willed her fortune and her home to her nephews, Hal and Larry, believing them to be promising young boys. Both her house and money were to be held in trust for them until Hal had turned twenty-three and Larry twenty-one. At that time it would only be released to them if they had developed a comprehensive and well-thought-out business plan through which they would invest the funds in partnership with one another, thus keeping alive the spirit of family enterprise for which the Schiffleys had been famous for generations. This plan had come alive for them during their college days at Harvard, where they had met my grandfather and begun a close intellectual and business association that lasted until the end of the Second World War. The Schiffleys and my grandfather had parted ways after a sharp disagreement over the philosophical underpinnings of the Marshall Plan, to which my grandfather was, of course, a major contributor. The disagreement over the Marshall Plan ended up causing an irreparable rift in their long and fruitful association.

After they came into their inheritance, the two boys occupied the house on the right for a time until they each married. At that point Hal moved into the house on the left. In their later years, after they had broken ties with my grandfather, they became increasingly reclusive and eccentric, shunning the company of persons not related to them. It was at this point that they elected to build an addition that would connect their two houses. Lucinda informed me that it was the belief of the chief curator that this connective passageway was actually built because Larry Schiffley's agoraphobia had becoming increasingly crippling in his later years. The passageway allowed him to visit his brother's family without leaving the house.

The dispute about the Marshall Plan had stemmed from the belief on the part of the Schiffley brothers that the plan would make America look too soft in the eyes of the world, and that the United States government should deal more firmly with both its enemies and allies alike. This belief that America was being made to look soft gave way to what has been cited by biographers as a full-blown paranoia with regard to the possibility of the imminent demise of the United States government in the face of increased immigration, fewer prolonged military engagements and what they felt to be a foreign service and Fulbright Commission excessively influenced by

French philosophy, turning diplomats from military envoys into decadent courtiers.

In order to shield themselves from the fall of the state, they famously reinforced the walls of their home, installing peepholes suitable for snipers just under the eaves of the house, stockpiling supplies of water and canned food sufficient for a siege lasting up to two years, and replacing their classic Philadelphia wooden shutters with bulletproof replicas. By the seventies, the Schiffleys no longer trusted the stock or bond markets, seeing them as appendages of a weak and effeminate state, and withdrew their entire fortune, famously causing a week-long crash that sent Wall Street reeling. They then converted their now liquid assets to gold bullion, and stored it in heavy bullet-proof chests under heavy security in the basement of Hal Schiffley's house.

The Fulbright Commission had become a particular cause for ire and indignation on the part of Hal Schiffley when his favorite daughter, Minnie, had received a Fulbright fellowship to study at the newly formed Africa Rice Center in Liberia in the early seventies. Hal Schiffley was enraged at his inability to stop Minnie from going to Africa and by the fact that the United States government was paying her to do it, thus making it impossible for him to refuse to pay for the 'African safari', as he apparently called it in a postcard to Minnie (now in the archive), according to Lucinda. It would probably have made him no happier to learn that Minnie went on to become one of the world's foremost experts on sustainable agriculture in the developing world. In my early teens, I had developed an infatuation with Dr. Minerva Green of the University of Wisconsin, Madison, when I learned from my mother that she was the daughter of one of the famous Schiffley brothers, who had been my grandfather's greatest enemies. Minnie Schiffley was born just after the war, and so my mother had never had a chance to meet her, a fact about which she always spoke with deep regret.

It had become my fantasy, when my mother had shown me an article in an issue of the *New York Review of Books* devoted to Africa that cited ground-breaking research on sustainable development and rice farming written by Drs. Minerva and Harvey Green, that I would somehow impress Minnie Schiffley with my own revolutionary theories about agriculture. Once she had shown enthusiasm for the brilliance of my ideas, I would then reveal my origins to her and reunite the families at last, after decades of battle. This aspiration was fueled in part by my mother's despondency and nostalgia for the old days when the families were together (although she had been quite young at the time, and was possibly relying on the stories of her older siblings and her father), and partly by the magnificent person of Dr. Minerva Green herself, shown in a photograph accompanying the article wearing a linen safari jumpsuit, and surrounded by members of the rice growers' co-op she had helped found in the late seventies with the help of her husband and mentor, Dr. Harvey Green.

Dr. Harvey Green had been Minnie Schiffley's professor in graduate school and appeared to be significantly older and less attractive than she. Dr. Minerva Green had a hearty Amazonian look to her. In the photograph, which was admittedly black and white and grainy, she was tall and tanned, with long dark hair pulled back in a bun. Her arms looked muscular and her eyes held the camera's gaze in a look of disdain. I longed for her approval, and secretly hoped that I might persuade her to leave Dr. Harvey Green and take up with a brilliant scholar of agriculture much younger than herself. Though this event did in due course take place, it was not I who broke up the Greens (and in truth, I never did acquire the requisite academic credentials in agricultural studies), but a brilliant young Nigerian scholar on a Fulbright to the United States to study with Dr. Minerva Green.

Waxen grapes
(from memory)

3

A few days before we visited the archive, I became nervous that some of Minnie Schiffley's documents might also be present there. I feared that perhaps somehow my numerous letters outlining strategic plans for combating world hunger through agricultural initiatives in cooperation with the UN and local groups of farmers in Southeast Asia might somehow have made their way into the Schiffley House Archive. Though I no longer held out any hope for a possible union between myself and Minnie Schiffley, nor even felt any strong need to reunite our families, I felt something of a twinge of embarrassment at the thought of my own juvenilia making its way into these files which would some day be available for public record. I therefore questioned Lucinda at great length as to the scope and origins of the documents in the archives, and whether the curators had any acquisitions mandates which might lead them to request that Dr. Minerva Schiffley donate her own correspondence files to the archive or to make the archive a beneficiary in her will.

Lucinda seemed to relish this line of questioning and warmed to the explication of a subject dear to her heart. I had hoped to disguise my own fear of discovery and humiliation with the appearance of a genuine fascination for the nuances of the curatorial field, with special reference to archive maintenance and development. I believe I succeeded quite admirably. Lucinda supplied me with bits of information regarding her trade at every possible opportunity, and I came to learn quite a bit about document bequests, cross-referencing and acid-free filing materials, among other things, although now, when I think about it, my memory is a bit hazy on many of the points she made during that visit. I did, however, learn enough to satisfy myself that the interests, acquaintances and correspondence of the Schiffley brothers alone were so vast that the curators had had to limit the scope of their project to those documents that bore a direct relation to the lives of the brothers themselves. Thus, such items as correspondence between Minnie Schiffley and Hal Schiffley could be found in the archive, as with the postcards that had fascinated Lucinda between father and daughter during the Fulbright to Liberia. However, the personal and professional correspondence of Dr. Schiffley did not fall within the collections strategy of the curatorial team.

In 1987, directly following the death of Hal Schiffley, who, being of sterner constitution, had outlived his brother Larry, the CIA took possession of all of the Schiffley papers in

Schiffley House and classified them. This was something I had become aware of in the course of my research on my grandfather's views on technology, but prior to my visit to Philadelphia, I had never known the reason. During the course of my discussions with Lucinda I had occasion to ask her about the classification of the Schiffley papers and to learn how it had come about. Lucinda explained that the formation of the CIA in 1947 had been yet another cause for ire toward President Truman on the part of the Schiffley brothers. Because of their preference for an aggressive stance for America on the world stage, they felt that the CIA's preference for intelligence gathering through undercover and secret operations made the country look weak and effeminate.

Lucinda had seen a postcard written by Larry Schiffley to Harry Truman, on which he had scrawled:

> Women, children and dime store detectives sneak around looking for hints and clues. Men walk in the front door and ask for what's needed. If they don't hear what they need to, they have two fists to prove their right to know. –Larry

In a press conference held on the Schiffley House lawn just after the war, in what was to become a ritual for the brothers, they had read out a statement in which they said, addressing the president:

> Mr. President, we put you in office and we paid

for your war. Don't doubt for a minute that if you persist in the creation of institutions, such as the Central Intelligence Agency, that weaken the American spirit and image, we can take you right out of that office.

Their criticism of the CIA, the Department of State, and the Fulbright Commission, as well as American foreign policy in general, became so strident and outrageous over the years that officials in the CIA had retaliated by declaring the Schiffley's files classified government property upon their death. The CIA had then taken possession of the files, keeping them from the public eye for about fifteen years, until one of Larry Schiffley's daughters managed through her husband's powerful business connections successfully to lobby Pennsylvania's senators to bring about the declassification of the papers through a congressional act. The papers were then returned to the Schiffley House archive, to the elation of the curators there, who had had to make do with managing walking tours of the houses and cataloguing press clippings, pamphlets and other Schiffley ephemera.

The curious detail in this story was that once the archive had been returned to Schiffley House, it had remained under lock and key and was now no more public than it had been when it was classified. The entire collection had now been in residence at Schiffley House for over two years, but no outsider had yet seen any of the documents it contained. When I asked Lucinda why this had happened, she was vague on the topic.

"You'd have to ask my boss," She said. "Antoinette feels very strongly about our archive. She says it has to be protected. But I'm not really sure from what. You can ask her yourself."

"Perhaps I can ask her leading questions which will draw her out on the subject."

"Oh, that's not hard," laughed Lucinda knowingly. "It's like she's in love with the archive."

My interest was piqued with the notion of an eminent female curator who keeps important documents away from the public eye, perhaps because she is too attached to them. I continued to ask Lucinda questions about this phenomenon and how it might have come about. Later in the day, as we strolled through the campus looking at different buildings and the quadrangles, Lucinda explained something of the deeper nature of archivists to me.

"Archivists who work with collections like ours always choose sides and identify with particular figures whose documents we catalogue. Everyone has a favorite. Mine is Louisa Schiffley. Antoinette identifies with Larry Schiffley."

"How odd! Does each archivist have a favorite?"

"Yes, no one overlaps, I guess. It's funny when you think about it."

"Well what qualities do you think make each of you identify with particular people? Is it the same kinds of things?"

"I'm not sure about that. We don't talk about it on a psychological level, if that's what you mean."

"So few of these characters seem sympathetic, it's interesting you would feel such a bond with them, and in particular that your boss would be attached to such an unbalanced figure as Larry Schiffley."

"We don't see them that way, you know," said Lucinda. She fell silent then, and I wondered if I had said something to offend her.

"I just wonder what it is, what is it that makes you sympathetic?" I asked more tactfully.

Lucinda looked at me slightly suspiciously but was too interested not to answer. "You see, we see their side of things. No one else sees it, but we see it. The Schiffleys were outspoken against the government and all the important figures of their time, so biographers have not been kind, and people haven't seen their side."

"But how can they see their side if none of you will show it to anybody?"

"I can't explain. I told you, you have to ask Antoinette about that part. But the other thing, about sympathizing. You don't know what it's like. We read their letters, we look at their photographs. We have journal entries. We see it from their point of view. Antoinette keeps particular files of Larry Schiffley's on her desk all the time, and she keeps particular pieces of his furniture, from the house collection in her office, like his desk. She has all different pictures of him on her bulletin board. She actually knew him, too. Did I tell you that?"

"You didn't! How did she know him?"

"I'm not exactly sure how it happened, but I think Larry Schiffley knew her dad somehow. He might have even put her through college. You can ask her that, too."

I liked to think that perhaps I would be able to persuade this unusual woman to allow me to visit the archive. If I could gain access to the collection, my research on my grandfather would contain information no other previous biographer had seen.

Standard MacIntosh:
· tart
· slightly discolored

4

When we arrived at the Hal Schiffley house on Tuesday, we parked in the staff lot and went in through the back entrance. Avoiding the front part of the house, which was open for tours, we went up the staircase to the servants' quarters on the third floor of the house, which was now occupied entirely by the archive and the curators' offices. Little effort had been put into the decoration of these offices, and they appeared to have remained more or less as they had been before the house had become a museum. The third floor had small, oddly shaped rooms with slanted white slat ceilings. The walls were covered in wallpaper with small busy floral patterns. The furniture consisted of old metal office furniture, painted a gunpowder green. Antoinette had been informed of my visit and was expecting me in her office. Lucinda left me at the door. "You're not coming in?" I asked, surprised. "Oh, no," she said, "Antoinette doesn't like group meetings."

I knocked on the door, heard someone say, "Come in," and entered hesitantly. I was startled to see an African-American woman seated in a large armchair upholstered in rich Moroccan leather lined with brass studs at the seams. Her desk, an enormous roll-top affair covered with piles of old letters and photographs, was pushed up against the wall to one side. Her chair was next to a fireplace, unlit. The walls were painted a dark green color and displayed numerous framed photographs of what must have been multiple generations of Schiffleys, as well as some nineteenth-century hunting engravings.

Antoinette stood up to greet me, her hand held out stiffly to shake mine. Her words were friendly, but her demeanor was not. She was clearly suspicious of my intentions and not inclined toward sympathy. The cozy little meeting I had imagined in which I would convince a matronly old curator to let a young man go ahead and have a little peek at those interesting files faded away. Instead, my mind went into free-fall, as I struggled with warring urges to either retreat quickly from the room or put any and all tools at my disposal attempting to seduce this woman whose chilly demeanor did little to diminish her beauty.

Antoinette must have been in her mid-forties, and was quite tall, probably around five feet eleven inches, with the body and bearing of a long distance runner. She tied her hair back tightly in a large and magnificent pony tail which formed a halo around her head. By contrast, her clothing was rather dull and conservative. She wore a wraparound denim skirt that went down to her knees, a white ribbed turtleneck with a denim vest, and white woolen tights with black patent leather shoes. I must have stood staring at her rather longer than was appropriate. "Have a seat," she said brusquely and motioned toward an armchair that matched her own at the other side of the fireplace. I quickly sat down, perching uneasily at the edge of the seat; still wondering if I should flee at once, rather than face certain humiliation at the hands of this overwhelming archivist.

"Now," she said, crossing her legs and clasping her hands tightly around one knee, "How might I help you today?"

"Lucinda," I began, and then paused. "Lucinda is an old friend of mine, and she had suggested that I might speak with you about my grandfather and his relationship to the Schiffleys. It's a biography I'm thinking of writing about my grandfather. About his involvement with technology and things like that."

"Your grandfather." She responded. "Your grandfather and technology. And what would you expect to find in the Schiffley archive, exactly?"

I was at a loss. The connection no longer seemed clear to me, although I had never doubted it before. Everyone had understood it. It wasn't so much that everyone understood the connections I made when talking about my grandfather with regard to this project, but that they understood that when researching someone of the stature of my grandfather, there was never a question that every piece of information connected to him was important. To the rest of the world the Schiffleys were a pair of crackpots who had unwisely parted ways with him.

They had died in ignominy and shame as far as anyone else was concerned. The lasting Schiffley image emblazoned in the mind of the public was that of the armored treasury car sent by the IRS on the death of Hal Schiffley to pick up sufficient gold bullion from the basement to pay off thirty years of back taxes that the Schiffleys had refused to pay due to their disagreements with the government. Remaining well-connected to the end, they had managed to stay protected from imprisonment for tax evasion. After their deaths, their memory had been shamed and ridiculed by the public retrieval of their wealth on the part of the very government they had hated so much. And here I was, in front of this imposing woman, whose point of view so clearly differed from mine and that of the rest of the world that I began to doubt myself. To her, it was the Schiffley brothers who were the critical contributors to history, and my grandfather, revered by history, was an interloper. There was a long pause.

"I'm sorry," I said. "What I meant was, it's just that my grandfather and the Schiffleys worked so closely together on historically significant projects, such as the jet engine, and I have always thought that so much could be learned from their correspondence, and no one has seen it. I would like to be able to include it in this project."

"I'm not sure I understand," she responded coolly, "the precise nature of your project."

"Well, biographical, really. It's a biography."

"But how does this differ from all the other ones?"

"It's the technology part. I'm doing the technology angle.

It hasn't been looked at that much, I don't think. I thought I could do that part."

"You haven't seen my article, 'The Schiffley Brothers and the Spirit of Invention' then?"

"Well, no, but, that sounds really interesting. I would like to. Where could I find it?"

Antoinette rose and went over to a tall oak filing cabinet and pulled out the middle drawer. She flipped through and pulled out the article and handed it to me. It had been reprinted from an academic journal called *Invention: A journal of the study of invention, innovation and originality.*

"You can keep it," she said, fixing me with a hard stare.

This was clearly the key. It was a test to see if I was worthy enough to even discuss seeing the archive. I realized that I should not ask anything more of her for the moment.

"Thank you," I said. "Thank you very much. I will read this, and then, if you don't mind, I will be in touch to discuss the salient points."

"That would be fine." Though it could have been my imagination, I thought I sensed a softening in her view of me. It was probably not sufficient for me to ask her any other questions for the moment, but certainly enough to allow for the possibility of further conversation.

"I am leaving town tomorrow morning," I added. "But I will write to you after I have read your article."

"I will look for your letter," she replied, and held the door open for me. As I was halfway out the door, she added, "Make sure to have one of the docents give you a tour of the house.

It is a fine example of Edwardian architecture and neoclassical decoration."

I smiled and nodded, and then hurried down the hallway to Lucinda's desk.

"How did it go?" she asked.

"Great. It was great. She gave me an article she wrote." I held it out for her.

"Did you ask about the archive?"

"Yes. Well, sort of, but I think she wants me to read this first."

Lucinda smiled knowingly. "That's Antoinette," she said.

"You didn't tell me about her," I said.

"What do you mean?"

"About, you know, what she looks like and everything."

"You mean that she's black? I didn't?"

"No, you didn't, but that's not really what I mean, so much as that I didn't expect someone like her to be the person who identifies with Larry Schiffley. That's not the picture I had in my mind."

"She loves him."

"I can see that. But I saw something different, too. I saw that she sees them, the Schiffleys, in a way that we don't. I saw that she thinks of them as great men, whereas we think of them as lunatics, people you wouldn't respect."

"I don't see them that way, though."

"Okay, not you, but most people. I do, or did, but now I don't know. Anyway, I'm going to read this article and then talk to her about it."

"You mean you'll come back again?"

"I don't know. I'll write to her and then we'll see."

Lucinda looked slightly uneasy. "Okay then. Do you want to see the house?"

Lucinda would have an hour for lunch, so we arranged to go to a café nearby for sandwiches after I took the tour. Following lunch, I would take a taxi to the train station. As I set off to see the house, I little expected how much an ordinary tour of a stately home would impress my psyche so deeply.

5

Upon my return home from the trip to Philadelphia, I felt shaken and confused. It was always at moments like these, when I felt ill-equipped to clarify my thoughts, that an old urge would creep under my skin. If only I had access to just a small quantity of powder, I thought. Just enough to clear things up and get some perspective. I needed the proper tools to consider what I had seen at the Schiffley House. I needed help considering the fact of the fruit table. I also needed to read Antoinette's article, which somehow seemed a daunting task. It had been quite some time since I had indulged in my old vice, and I liked to think that I could easily make do without any assistance of that nature. I didn't especially wish to make the calls necessary to locate a modest portion of powder, but I often hovered near the phone in the days following my return from Philadelphia, trying to reason that a call would not be so difficult after all.

My partiality for powder had started in college during an adult stage of my lifelong avocation toward taste collection. As a young boy, I had collected tastes, the tastes of things I had eaten, or heard of someone eating, and things that could be drunk. Unlike other children, who recoiled in disgust at the very sight of new and unfamiliar foods, I relished and sought out such opportunities in order to add to my collection, no matter how repulsive a new taste sensation might be to me. Much to the chagrin of my parents, however, my willingness to experiment did not lead to a spirit of open-mindedness about the cuisines I had sampled. When engaging in games of one-upmanship with the parents of my contemporaries, my mother never mentioned the aftermath of my experiments.

On one occasion, I recall that I had seen an advertisement in the newspaper for a new Ethiopian restaurant in a neighboring town. I insisted that my parents take me to the restaurant as soon as possible, even though they themselves were not too keen on the new taste sensations that Ethiopian food might make available to them. The restaurant occupied the former premises of an Italian American establishment in a small, low-lying strip mall along a fairly busy section of a bypass route near the town next door. My parents were reluctant to dine in a strip mall, but they were proud of their son's adventuresomeness and wanted to make a go of it. Like a family of explorers, we set out for the Café Addis Ababa. The restaurant was near-deserted, although the parking lot was busy, due to the presence of two much larger and more successful businesses on the lot: a video rental store and a popular submarine sandwich shop.

We sat as far back in the restaurant as we could, away from the large plate glass windows looking out onto the bustling parking lot and the endless lines of cars whizzing by, in order, as my father put it, "To see if we can't pretend to be in some little dive in Ethiopia!" The new proprietors of the restaurant had done little to change the décor since their arrival. The walls were papered in a dark red and gold swirling pattern, and the sides of the room were lined with dark wooden booths, their seats upholstered in ketchup-red vinyl. Two chandeliers were suspended from the ceiling by heavy-looking link chains. Each light bulb was pointed, like a candle flame, and ensconced in a heavy gold glass floret, which caused them to cast a muted golden glow about the room. There were still maps of Italy on the walls and enlarged photographs mounted on foam board of Italian peasant women at harvest time carrying baskets of wheat and tomatoes. Over our table hung a floridly painted still life of a bowl of fruit with a bottle of wine. The paint was thickly layered onto what must have been an old mirror. My father, an art historian, groaned softly when he saw this, but managed to take the painting in stride for the duration of the meal. The tablecloths were red and white checked; even the china and glasses seemed to have been inherited from the previous owners.

I was in high spirits in anticipation of this new addition to my collection. I had never collected anything at all from Africa, and beyond an order of Chinese takeout acquired in Boston when we had gone there to visit the Museum, this was really my first foray outside the cuisines of the Americas and Europe. Over my parents' objections, I insisted we order everything on the menu, promising earnestly that I would personally be responsible for consuming all the leftovers we brought home.

The most thrilling moment of the evening was when the waiter brought out the large piece of cushiony bread (that we were all to share!), and carefully spooned out six small piles of food from six different dishes onto the bread. I was fascinated by the fact that each pile looked almost exactly like the other, especially with respect to color. This would require me to collect the tastes using my taste buds alone! I would have no help from visual cues, and no other way to remember the experience besides through my tongue. I had taken out a number of books from the library on the different tastes experienced by the different areas of the tongue and this meal would represent my first opportunity to put into practice what I had read, in the total absence of familiarity, expectation or visual data. It was to be a true scientific experiment.

I had already taken out my taste collection diary and fountain pen, and written down the names of all the dishes we had ordered. When the waiter had finished serving us, I asked him to identify each pile by name, and then I drew a diagram of the bread and the food on the bread, each item properly labeled. My parents sat by silently, not sure if they should dig in before my diagram was done, or how they should interpret my behavior for the waiter. My mother laughed nervously and looked up at the waiter. "It's a class project," she said. "Foods of the world." The waiter stared blankly at her and then smiled warily. He was not sure if he should go away or if I was going to require more information of him. Looking at the clock, he held the tray behind his back and shifted from one foot to the other. When I had finished my writing, I looked up at him and said firmly, "Thank you." That seemed to be enough and he went away.

The time to initiate the collection had arrived. Being at that time quite short for my age, my face was close to the food. The steam from the different piles, or curries, as my father called them, fogged up my glasses, thus reducing reliance on my visual faculties even further. This, in turn, augmented the sensation that I was embarking on my collection project, which was also part experiment, in Plato's cave. The story of Plato's cave had been read to me from an authoritative translation of the ancient Greek by my uncle Ned, a 'non-union scholar of Classics,' as he called himself, following a large Thanksgiving meal which had rendered everyone but him and me incapable of speech or interaction for a good three hours. During that time, Uncle Ned, in an exceedingly gregarious mood (due to excessive alcohol consumption, according to my mother), undertook to give me, at the age of eight, a solid grounding in the Classics. I was so flattered that I had been chosen for this indoctrination, as he termed it, on the very basis of our civilization, that I didn't want to interrupt him in the flow of his readings and explications. Thus, to this day, the power of that indoctrination, and my hazy understanding of much of what I was told, continues to muddle my perception of many of the basic tenets of Greek and Roman philosophy, mythology and history, despite the best efforts of subsequent preceptors.

It was thus that I had developed an understanding of Plato's cave as something to do with the optimal conditions under which an experiment should be conducted. The men sitting in the cave were there to study the human condition. By doing so with their backs to the distracting swirl of sensations represented by immersion in every day life, they had achieved a greater degree of objectivity. They watched the silhouettes, or shadows, of humankind intently as they faced inside the cave. The movement of these shadows presented them with certain objective truths that would not have been available to them under normal circumstances. And so I approached my Ethiopian taste collection project in a manner which fairly reduplicated the objectivity of the scientists in Plato's cave, though of course, there was still the troubling notion of the interaction between taste buds and smell, the latter of which I was not entirely sure I should yet forego, though later experiments with more familiar tastes were to involve clamping my nose shut with a clothespin.

The waiter had placed five piles in a circle and the sixth at the center. I decided to begin at the top of the circle, at twelve o'clock, and then proceed clockwise, ending up in the middle. I took a small spoonful off the pile at twelve o'clock and placed it on my plate. I also tore off a small section of the bread and placed it beside the spoonful of food. My parents tried to convince me to eat the food with the bread as a scoop, as we had seen a couple of diners across the restaurant doing. I refused, however, believing this to be less scientific than eating each item separately. The first spoonful of food, along with each subsequent spoonful, was unremittingly spicy, no doubt due to what I believed to be chili peppers, a substance I had only read about. I had no tolerance for hot food, which meant that this experiment would require a steely resolve. I catalogued the results of each bite on my diagram, and below, where I had a notes section. Wiping the steam from my glasses, and blinking through the tears of pain, I carefully noted degrees of hotness for each item and attempted to describe the experience of my taste buds, carefully moving bites of food from one area of my tongue to the next.

My parents, after some misgivings, had decided that they were happy with the food and were busily making their way through their dinners. They were accustomed to my collecting of tastes and talked between themselves, every now and then gazing anxiously over at me, notebook spread out, eyes watering with pain, glasses smudged, my plate covered with small dabs of food carefully placed so as not to run into one another and taint the discreet tastes that were entering my collection. By the time I had completed my project, I felt overwhelmed with waves of nausea that could barely be controlled. "Are you all right, dear?" my mother asked. "He looks a little pale...." my father said. By then I was sure I was going to vomit. My mother waved for the check and my father led me out of the restaurant into the parking lot, which was full of video store patrons pulling in and out of parking spots. Seeing my mort ification at the thought of vomiting in front of so many people, my father took me behind a large dark green dumpster at the side of the complex where I promptly disgorged my entire meal, as well as the balance of the contents of my stomach.

6

In the heyday of my taste collecting exercises, the connection between the faculties of taste and smell had always bothered me. I had, of course, learned to tame the sense of smell by blocking my nostrils in various ways while I endeavored to experience the unadulterated sensation of the food in contact with my taste buds. But in college, where I was for the first time living in a city, the notion of smell began to intrigue me, as I found that each day I stepped out into the urban environment was a new and riotous experience for my sense of smell. A collection of smells, not so systematically collected as the tastes of my younger efforts due to the constraints on my time from college as well as maintaining an acceptable level of social activity, gave way to an interest in the notion of 'eating' or ingesting substances through the nostrils.

After spending so much time attempting to isolate the taste buds from the sense of smell, I began to wonder if I had only learned half the story by privileging the tongue over the nose. Unable to imagine a way that one could mask the experience of the taste buds effectually, I resolved instead to explore the world of nasal ingestion. This idea came to me one evening when I was self-administering a nasal spray in my ongoing battle with the many and various airborne pollens and other substances that I count among my enemies. Of course, I thought, there are many substances that are meant to be taken through the nostrils. I resolved to do some research on the subject and soon my interest grew in the taking of snuff, as well as the collection of snuff-related paraphernalia.

My interest in snuff, which did become a habit for a time, gave me a certain reputation about campus. This in turn led to a surprising number of invitations to gatherings of a somewhat exclusive nature. I found that unlike the collection habits of my childhood, which had set me apart from other children as peculiar and bookish, this collection of nasal sensations made me tremendously popular among a certain set, and where before I had had to work diligently to maintain and acquire friendships and associations that were not particularly prepossessing, I was now sought out and my company was desired. Everyone in these groups had intriguing qualities and unusual interests. There were many interested in history and antique clothing and furniture. There were also quite a few dabblers in the occult arts and a number of painters, sculptors, playwrights and so on. The parties were delightful, and often some type of period costume was required for special evenings; for example, a particular individual's birthday might be celebrated in the aesthetic of a Pre-Raphaelite painting, or a New Year's party would be put on as a *Bal Masqué*.

Those were happy days, and, although I did not have any great talent to contribute to the mix as so many of my associates did, I did have a wealth of knowledge regarding tastes and smells due to my collections, as well as an ability to help with the research for the period settings of the parties. I felt at the time, and I still believe, that I was considered a valued contributor to the circles in which I moved, and a not unamusing conversationalist.

There were those of my group who were attached to consuming alcohol and other mind-altering drugs at our parties. At first I kept aloof from these practices, and only took alcohol or an occasional puff of tobacco in order to satisfy my intellectual curiosity about their tastes. I did begin to develop a taste for certain types of wines and liqueurs, but never felt the need to sample them to excess, preferring to savor the ports and sherries slowly as I rolled their rich syrups carefully from one region of my tongue to the other in the manner in which I had trained myself earlier in life. At that time I also began my collection of fine glassware and decanters to help with the consumption of wines and liqueurs.

At some point during my final year in college, our parties began to reach new heights of decadence, or so it seemed to me. I could scarcely have imagined such gatherings in my more reclusive underclassman days. Liquor flowed freely, and powder, heroin, hallucinogenic mushrooms and even opium seemed available in abundance. Factions began now to grow within our group as to the appropriateness of some of these substances at our parties. I was of a group that maintained that some of these were aesthetically unsuitable for the themes of the parties. Opium and other historically interesting drugs fell into the category of fine alcoholic beverages with significant historical weight, but the newer drugs, such as heroin or powder, seemed crassly inappropriate in our carefully orchestrated theme parties. Numerous and vociferous arguments broke out on such occasions, often under the influence of the entire range of substances being ingested at the time, and there were even occasional fist-fights, as well as one challenge to a duel that thankfully never came to fruition.

I was at that time quite drawn to a newer member of our group who had been spending a year studying art history in Rome and had only recently joined our number. Roger Pencil was a talented painter and poet with a dashing sense of style. He was always extremely well dressed, even if his clothing had been picked up from a thrift shop. He sported a thin mustache and kept his hair slicked back. His luck with women led some jealous rivals to suspect him of being a practitioner of the dark arts, or at the very least a cad, but those close to him understood that his charm came from simply not caring about anything. His main passions were for Italian painting, British Romantic poetry, and chemically induced intoxication. His two chief intoxicants were the Greek liquor, ouzo, and powder.

Roger and I were in a number of classes together and lived in the same apartment building, just off Harvard Square. I had invited him over a few times after spending many interesting hours in coffee shops hearing about his adventures in Italy and his strong identification with the Romantic poets. I think he grew to respect me when I served him a dinner consisting of a number of tastes I believed I had managed to isolate over the years into pure, distilled sensations. His chilly aloofness seemed slowly to melt under the influence of a few bottles of good wine, and I was surprised to find that his love of art and poetry was firmly rooted in a passionate and articulate heart. It was a perception of this passion, perhaps, which drew so many women to him; perhaps they intuited the soothing warmth at his core and hoped somehow to reach it and bask in its rays.

Roger and I discovered that we had remarkably similar taste in literature and the arts, and despite our very different personalities, we found we always had much to discuss in this regard. We were both great believers in the Romantic poets, but did not care for the Modernists. While finding the paintings of Lucian Freud oddly mesmerizing, we could not abide Picasso, especially his later work. In the first flush of our friendship we shared views I had held since my childhood: details that I had never told anyone, about my love for the Flemish painters, or my preference for the plays of Beaumarchais over their opera adaptations, or the transcendent quality of audio recordings of Sarah Bernhard as Phèdre.

Over the next few weeks I enjoyed his company at all times except for those occasions on which he indulged himself in his fondness for powder. At such times his chill became tangible and I felt my closeness to him slip away until I was separated from him as though by several layers of glass. I could see him and hear him, but I could not reach him. Roger with powder could be even more impressive than Roger without it.

One evening when I had invited him over for dinner, I hesitantly began what became a series of debates between the two of us on the subject of his use of the drug. At first I was all affront, and unable to concede a single point he made in his effort to convince me of the benefits of using powder. But gradually his persuasive arguments began to win me over and I found myself intrigued. His first argument appealed to the collector in me.

"Your experiments," he said.

"Yes?"

"Cocaine fits directly into your experiments."

"How so?"

"Isn't it obvious?" he chuckled. "Isn't it obvious that if you haven't tried this drug, your collection of nasal sensations is incomplete?"

"But how can it fit into the collection? It is an unappealing substance. The idea doesn't please me. It doesn't fit with the other items in the collection."

"I don't see how you can make that claim. You have told me of so many unappealing substances that you have eaten or ingested through your nose. In my opinion, far better cocaine than inhaling liquids into your nose through a straw just to test the sensations of the nasal cavity."

"True...." I had to concede that appealingness was not actually a criterion for my collecting principles.

"You are applying your aesthetic standards for social activity to this question, rather than the far more scientific standards you apply to your collecting." Roger paused to take a sip of ouzo and munch on a medjool date, which I had served for dessert for its nearly perfectly pure taste.

"That's a good point," I conceded. We were silent for a moment. Then I continued, "but I am concerned that the mind-altering component of the drug will overpower the nasal sensation and make it difficult to separate the two, just as taste and smell are difficult to separate."

"That doesn't seem to be a concern for you with liquor," he pointed out.

"True, but I don't drink much liquor."

"Well then you could choose the same approach with the coke," he pointed out.

"I see, yes. I see what you mean. Still, it worries me. The effects will be unusual and they will possibly cloud my judgment."

"That remains to be seen, does it not? Isn't that the spirit of the experiment?"

"It's not an experiment, not really. It's a collection, remember?"

"Yes, of course, but there is an element of experiment to the process as you have explained it to me."

"Yes, of course, you are right. There is an element."

We spoke of it no more that evening but soon after I resolved to ingest the substance just once. I did so when we two were alone. I took only a little, but I was shocked and a little embarrassed by the pleasing quality of the mind-altering component of the drug. I realized that I had understood mind-altering to mean 'mind-muddling', as was often the case of the effect of alcohol on the brain. This drug, by contrast, afforded me a startling and unforeseen access to clarity of thought. It was a clarity that I had often longed for when musing on my collections. The sensation quickly became precious and exciting to me.

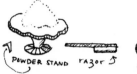

POWDER STAND   razor   hand mirror

7

From that point on, I used the drug to clarify my thoughts and aid me in my collection projects. I experienced its effects as illuminating. I found myself more able to separate the disparate elements of a taste or a s mell, or simply write an essay for an assignment or solve a mathematical equation. I never took the drug on social occasions, but it became known in our circles that I had crossed a line without really relinquishing my original stance, and this caused no small degree of discomfort with my companions. Some friends even took me aside to confront me, saying they no longer knew where I stood. They were not altogether satisfied when I explained that I used the drug only as an aid in learning the truth about the qualities of certain things that were important to me. Lucinda had been of this group. Never a great fan of Roger Pencil, she saw this development as evidence that I had somehow fallen under his sway. On several occasions she begged me to stop and would not listen to my reasoning.

Several years after college, I was forced to admit that perhaps, despite myself, I had developed something of a habit. Then ensued the usual tedious rounds of interventions by friends, distasteful meetings in murky little church basements and so forth. Since then, I have been more or less 'clean' as they say in the parlance of substance abuse programs. Though Lucinda and other friends of that circle persist in using this language when talking to me, I maintain that the problem was never so great as they seemed to think, and that I was not so much addicted to the substance per se, as to the clarity of vision with which it provided me. And I have, unbeknownst to them, continued to occasionally and judiciously use this drug whenever I felt that it was greatly needed for achieving moments of clarity.

It was to Roger that I had invariably turned whenever I felt the need for some powder. I wanted to call him now, but Roger had changed, and a series of events had made it increasingly difficult to gain access to the Roger Pencil who had been so important to me in college and later. Principally, Roger had fallen in love with, and then married, Anne Rhinestone, a modern dancer. Anne had been part of our group in college, but generally associated with the other faction of the group. In those days, she was a ballet dancer as well as an art history major. She often arranged dance performances for the more elaborate parties and favored the Art Nouveau period both in her studies and her sense of style. There was something of the flapper about Anne, and there hung about her an air of cultivated aloofness.

Anne had recognized the attractions of Roger and, choosing not to join the cloud of admiring girls that buzzed about his person at all times, she had waited and bided her time. Anne was skilled at long-range planning, and the acquisition of Roger Pencil was a particularly illuminating example of this quality in her. In time, Roger became fascinated by this exquisitely beautiful and poised woman who appeared to want nothing to do with him. I had been distantly acquainted with Anne since secondary school (though I was never in her league in those days) and recognized her characteristic seduction style early on in her pursuit of Roger. I attempted to warn Roger, but he was neither convinced that she had any interest in him, nor that if she did he should maintain an attitude of caution toward her. Taking his cue from his favorite poets, he did not think much of caution in love, and so my warnings fell on deaf ears.

Anne succeeded in the end, and just around the time she was switching over to modern dance and had cut her hair short, Roger had finally, he felt, persuaded her to take an interest in him. The first time he managed to stay the night at her apartment was the night of her now well-known interpretation of *Swan Lake* set to the music of Thelonius Monk. I attended that historic performance with Roger, but could barely concentrate as I watched the shades of fascination and adoration wash across his face in the semidarkness of the theater. I knew then that Anne had captured him and that she would never let him go. We had gone backstage to congratulate her and found her surrounded by admiring fans and reporters. She looked triumphant, but I suspected that the source of that look was Roger's attitude of abject devotion, rather than the standing ovation she had just received. Momentarily turning away from the reporters, she looked straight into Roger's eyes. Her gaze was like a spear. It left no room for me. I shuffled out of the theater through a side door. Initially it had been my thought to get some air, but when the door closed and I noticed it was locked from the outside, I took it as a sign, and slowly made my way through the falling snow to the train.

That night had been bitingly cold. Back in my apartment, I wrapped myself in a quilt and sat in an armchair at the window overlooking the street. I first drank port, then moved onto snuff and finally resorted to the sniffing of powder, despite the fact that a lucid emotional state was the last thing I wanted. I then returned to the port and took to aimlessly cataloguing my snuffboxes in a new bound diary I had bought for that purpose. At three in the morning I had called Lucinda and woken her from a deep sleep. "Go to sleep," she had told me. "You're high, I can tell you're high. Sleep it off and call me tomorrow." It was unsatisfactory. She had not been sympathetic.

From then on Roger had always been with Anne and of Anne. His clothing changed, his habits changed, his interests changed. His once threadbare secondhand suits and cravats, carefully selected at the Salvation Army, were replaced with neater clothing that had the more modern look Anne preferred. He was obliged, it seemed, to take up an interest in dance, which he did with gusto, and was rarely available for the musical performances and art shows we had often attended together in the past. Most perturbingly, where once he could easily be located during the course of the day at a certain café or a particular bookstore, it became difficult to find him anywhere without arranging things beforehand. It felt unpleasant to make what amounted to an appointment with such a dear friend. Roger now referred always to 'we' and never 'I.' The only time we spent together was when Anne was on tour; now that there were children, these precious moments had grown even fewer.

All the same, unbeknownst to Anne, the old Roger still existed in nooks and crannies of his being. He was a secret poet, a secret philanderer and a secret user of intoxicants. He still knew where to purchase his favorite drugs and every once in a while he would tell Anne he had to go out of town for work, whereupon he rented a hotel room on the other side of town and wrote poetry. Occasionally he issued forth from these sojourns to a bar and, once more the dashing wolf, effortlessly attracted some young lady. Sometimes he called me at an odd time and invited me to join him for a drink, or to meet him for breakfast with one of his 'new friends' after a night of carousing. These were the only occasions at which one could truly get a glimpse of the old Roger. Of course I always went.

After I had returned from Philadelphia, I hesitated for

some time before deciding to call Roger. He would not be pleased, but it could not be helped. I had never been comfortable buying intoxicants from vendors in the streets, and Roger always seemed to know which sellers could be trusted. And so I dialed his number. Roger answered.

"Hello?" I was glad it was he who had answered and not Anne.

"Roger." I said. "I need some powder. I'm sorry to call you so late and at home, but something has happened and I really need it."

There was a silence. He was not pleased. He sighed. "Look, can't we talk in the morning?" he asked.

"No," I said. "This can't wait. Something has come up and it requires thought. Clear thought."

"Hold on." He went through the process of going into another room and replacing the phone on its cradle in the first room. Then he came back, speaking in a whisper.

"You can't call me in the middle of the night like this, I told you that."

"I'm sorry. I'm really sorry."

"And you can't ask me for coke when Anne is lying asleep next to me. If she knew, I don't know what she'd do!"

"I'm sorry, Roger, I'm really sorry, it's just that..."

"Okay, okay. I can leave some for you in the green tin on the back porch. But be very quiet when you come. And please understand that I can't take it with you. I'll be going back to bed."

"Roger?"

"Yes, what?"

"It's just that something has come up. There was a table in a house and I have to think about it. You know I wouldn't ask if it wasn't an emergency."

"I know, I know. You just put me in an awkward position, that's all. I understand. I'll leave it out for you. I have to go now. You'll be okay, right?"

"Yes, thanks. I'm really grateful to you. I'm sorry I woke you."

I put my boots and coat back on and went outside and stood on the sidewalk in front of my building for a few moments. It was quite cold. I practiced breathing deeply, in and out, to feel the air come into my nose and then watch the smoke of my breath escape slowly in puffs into the still of the darkness. It was a ritual I practiced at moments of great tension. Then I pulled my collar and scarf about me and set out to walk the ten blocks to Roger and Anne's.

When I reached their house, I walked slowly and quietly up the steps to the green tin. Roger had left enough for me to get through this thinking process for two evenings. He always understood how much I needed. I put the bag in my pocket and slowly replaced the lid of the tin so as not to make any noise. This had become our routine. He always protested, but he was a loyal friend to me at such times. I walked down the steps again to the sidewalk and turned to face their house. I stood and stared at the darkened windows for a few minutes, all the while engaged in my breathing ritual. The cold was bitter, and ice formed about my nostrils. Finally, I turned away and walked swiftly back to my apartment where I might undertake the necessary thought for decoding the questions that so troubled my mind.

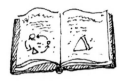

8

A month or so after I had returned from Philadelphia, I was seated in a café reading the newspaper. At some point, a crowd of students walked through the door, bringing with them a rush of cold air. I looked up, and noticed a board on which were tacked numerous flyers advertising goods and services, as well as announcements of events. Protruding out from under some newer flyers, I thought I saw the name 'Dr. Antoinette Garner'. I immediately made my way over to the notice board, removed the flyers that obscured the one that bore that name and seized it, taking the flyer back to my seat for closer examination. It was an announcement for a lecture by Dr. Antoinette Garner, to be given at a nearby university. The lecture was to be the next day at 5 p.m. I was perplexed by the title: "The Fortunate Experiment: Prison Writings from the Philadelphia House of Correction 1973–1978." Could this be the same Dr. Antoinette Garner? Sure enough, in smaller letters at the bottom, a brief biography of the speaker was included:

> Dr. Antoinette Garner is the Curator-in-Chief
> at the Schiffley House Museum and Archives in
> Philadelphia, PA. She received her PhD in 1999
> from the University of Pennsylvania's Department
> of Sociology. She writes on prison writing pro-
> grams and various topics relating to the Schiffley
> House archives.

I was taken aback by the apparent incongruity of Antoi-
nette's specialization in prison writing with her occupation
as head curator of the Schiffley House archives. Since return-
ing from Philadelphia, I had read her article "The Schiffley
brothers and the Spirit of Invention." It had been informative,
though dry, and I had planned to write her a carefully worded
note on the subject sometime soon. This I had been putting
off, however, out of an anxiety that I might take some wrong
step in my interaction with her to cause her to judge me un-
worthy of viewing the archives. Seeing the flyer and reflecting
on the possibility of seeing her in person again reminded me
of another source of anxiety, namely, the attraction I had felt
to her and my secret hope that I might somehow impress her
enough through my respect for the significance of the Schiff-
ley House archives to make her take a similar interest in me.

I resolved that I must go to the lecture. Hurriedly finish-
ing my cup of coffee, I gathered up my things and made my
way to the local library to research Antoinette's other work on

prison writing. If I was to go to the lecture, I would need to be prepared.

Later that night I sat at my desk and lit the oil lamp I keep there. I felt restless and got up again and went to the kitchen to pour myself a glass of scotch. Then I went back and sat down to gather my thoughts and peruse the information I had attained in my research on the work of Dr. Antoinette Garner. I had been quite thorough that day. An entire pad full of notes lay open before me. I have always preferred to take notes in an even hand, where possible, but on this occasion I had felt rushed. Each page was covered with a hasty cursive scrawl, a tangle of observations, page numbers and citations. I had not had my wits about me. On such occasions it is my practice to re-copy my notes into a fresh copy book with pen and ink. This allows me to preserve them, as well as affording me the opportunity to reorganize and re-evaluate my thoughts for further information gathering.

Now, however, something did not feel right. I sat still for several minutes, the glass of scotch on a brass coaster at the right corner of the writing desk, my right hand hovering above the new notebook, pen poised and at the ready, left hand holding down the pages of tangled notes. Carefully replacing the pen on its stand, I stood up and walked across the room to the record player. I selected the *Moonlight Sonata* and placed it on the turntable. Once the music began, I went to my closet and took my flannel robe from the hook on the back of the closet door. The robe and the *Moonlight Sonata* would bring about a peace of mind needed to prepare my nerves for attending the lecture the following day. I lacked composure.

I returned to my writing desk, took a sip of whiskey, and braced my hands on the table. I pressed my palms on the paper, on each side of the open notebook. Antoinette was a well-known scholar of prison writings. I closed my eyes. The interior of Schiffley House appeared. The secret passageways of the Annex, the dark, brooding interior rooms, the heavy furnishings and the fruit table. Over the past month, with the help of the powder attained from Roger, and then without, I had slowly trained my memory to erase the Schiffley House docent from both the visual and audial memory of the tour. The process was one I had begun to develop in my childhood in my early collections. I had slowly perfected it over time. In the case of tastes, I had used it both while acquiring the tastes, and later, when recopying my notes, to eradicate imperfections and aid in the distillation of pure sensation. Some friends had likened the process to meditation, but I have always felt it is more active than that. Many rousing exchanges have occurred at parties and in cafés on the topic, but I have always maintained that my thought exercises are the absolute opposite of meditation, as they involve an acutely active state of cogitation and have often induced states in me quite contrary to relaxation. I have heard it argued by aficionados of meditation that that activity is also quite active in nature, but no one has been able to counter my argument that my thought exercises produce in me an almost unbearable state of excitement.

Concentrating deeply, I moved slowly through a series of images of the Schiffley House interior. When I arrived at the fruit table, the point to which I travel each time I attempt the exercise, I felt a shiver run down my spine. In my mind's eye, for the first time, I saw what I had been looking for, what I had been working towards. The fruit table stood before me, absolutely static, but the room changed back and forth, back and forth, altering its appearance with the insistent pace of the blinking of a neon light. This continued for a number of minutes before I managed to cause the pace of the alterations to go more slowly. Only at the point at which they slowed down sufficiently for me to see what was on the other side of the Schiffley interior, what image it alternated with, did I at last know what it was that had been eating away at me ever since I had left Philadelphia.

The other image was that of my grandparents' living room. As the images shifted back and forth, the table remained immobile. Of course I had known from the start that the presence of the fruit table in Schiffley House, identical in every way to the table I had known growing up, would perplex and fascinate me for some time to come. There was no surprise there. The information that had proved so elusive, however, was what the sameness of two tables told me about the difference between two rooms. Reviewing my thoughts and my notebooks, over and over again, the darkness and Victorian qualities of Schiffley House had struck me in a particular way.

There was something unexpected about it, despite the fact that such an interior, such a series of small, close chambers admitting only minimal sunshine, should be expected in the Philadelphia home of a prominent family such as the Schiffleys. Now I knew why this décor and ambience had arrested my attention. It was because of what it told me about the interior of my grandparents' home.

The fruit table in the Schiffley House belonged utterly to the room where it had been housed for over a century. The fruit table in my grandparents' house had never belonged in the room where I had encountered it. That room, the drawing room, had been done up, as I have mentioned, in a very modern style. The palette was light and spanned a number of subtle hues all in pale yellows, mustards and beiges. The shapes in that room had been of simple, geometric design, the art on the walls abstract and strictly non-representational. What an anomaly was the fruit table! It had always been my understanding, though upon reflection, perhaps based on nothing more than youthful impressions, that my grandparents' house had been decorated in the fifties by a professional, and was not the organic outcome of an accumulation of objects and tastes jumbled together in the manner one finds in most houses. My mother's mother, who had been my grandfather's third wife, had passed away some years before. The house I had known was purchased by my grandfather a short time prior to his courtship and marriage to his fourth wife, Grand Jane, the owner of the fruit table.

With my envisioning of the images of the two rooms

superimposed upon one another, I had stumbled upon a deep-seated, unconscious question. This question, I now realized, had long been a source of anxiety to me since childhood, namely: why had my grandparents decorated their house in that manner? It might seem trivial, initially, to consider such a question, but in point of fact, it resulted from a sensation I had experienced when I was quite young that my grandparents did not quite belong in their house, and particularly not in that room. Though I am aware that sitting rooms, especially those reserved for formal calls, often have the chilly, impersonal feel to them of a waiting room at a doctor's office or the reception area of a hotel, there was something about my grandparents' entire house that suggested not a home, but a stage set or a showcase.

Now I realized the fruit table in Louisa Schiffley's drawing room had told me something about my grandparents' house: something about belonging. The fruit table had been the one object I remembered fondly from that house, and yet it had not belonged there. It did belong somewhere and it did belong to someone. Perhaps this was what it had signaled to me as a child: connectedness. It had belonged in fact to my grandmother and had traveled with her from her previous life, before us. I wondered if I had perceived at that time that it was connected to her, or if I had merely discerned that it was endowed with a quality of connectedness in some innate manner. This was a quality that did not exist between the people and the objects, or even within the objects throughout the rest of the house. It was perhaps one of the few items in the house that had a history. The fact remained, however, that we did not have any idea where and how my grandmother had come by the table, and where it had gone, following her death. It was odd how little, on reflection, I seemed to know about her family, her past and her connections. It was also odd that this table had entered our family after the rift had occurred between my grandfather and the Schiffley brothers, as my grandfather's fourth marriage occurred after the break in ties. Thus, I surmised, there could be no question of the two tables having some connection through the close association of the two families.

The fact that my grandparents' house had been purchased and decorated in a modern style following the rift with the Schiffleys also troubled me. This was the other piece of information that the twin fruit tables were trying to convey to me in my envisioning. How had my grandfather lived before that house? Because of the table, I now realized that the style of décor and architecture did not originate from my grandmother's tastes. Certainly, on reflection, she had never seemed comfortable there. Had he changed interior design with each new wife? I could not help but feel that he was somehow hiding something by choosing that house and its contents. It was a showcase, certainly, but a showcase could also be a kind of costume. I wondered if he had inhabited some kind of Schiffley House in earlier years that I had not been told of. His move into the house I knew so well did coincide with his growing fame and prosperity, which might account for its artificiality. I am sure he was not the first man to seek a new setting in which to showcase his life and his genius in a time of increasing prominence and affluence.

9

I had probably been seated at my desk for over an hour, perfectly still, in an attitude of absolute concentration, when suddenly my doorbell rang. My concentration broke and I startled. It was a nervous reaction I was used to, as it invariably occurred whenever some loud noise or other stimulus reached me while I was envisioning something. The shock and surprise of my broken concentration seemed always to cause in me a series of involuntary gestures as well as, on occasion (I have been told), incoherent speech acts. On this occasion, my glass of scotch ended up on the floor, though thankfully the glass was not broken. I had by this time forgotten the cause of my inquietude and gone to the kitchen sink to bathe my face in cold water, a gesture which soothes my nerves at such times.

Again the doorbell rang. This time I was cognizant of the noise and what it meant. Going to the intercom, I enquired as to who was below. It was Roger, who was in the habit of showing up at my apartment at odd times when Anne was on tour with her company. Was this one of those times? It must be. I could not immediately recall if I had known this or not, though it was probable that I did. I buzzed Roger in and waited at the open door, hands at my sides, staring at the ivy patterned wallpaper at the far side of the hallway. Roger came up. He looked at me oddly and patted me on the shoulder before removing his snow-covered hat, coat, muffler and boots. He was wearing a maroon wool suit and plum colored shirt. When he removed his boots, I noted that his socks had clocks on them.

"What's wrong? What do you have going on in here?" he asked.

"I was concentrating on the table," I explained. "Where did you find those socks?"

"These? They were my grandfather's," he said. He looked around the room thoughtfully and I followed his gaze. The record was spinning around and around on the phonograph, the needle dragging and scratching at the inner grooves. The scratching made a rhythmic sound. He looked at my glass of scotch on the floor, and a candle, burned nearly to the bottom, with wax dripping rapidly onto the windowsill and over the edge onto the floor.

"I surprised you," he said. "I'm sorry."

"It's fine. Nothing can be done about it, really. You didn't know."

"Sit down and I'll bring you a fresh drink."

I sat down in an armchair and Roger put a plaid blanket over me. Then he poured us each a scotch and rummaged about in my cabinets for something to eat. I watched him do this and wondered what time it was. I hoped I had not lost any information from my session, as I usually took notes directly afterwards. Now Roger was here, and I would have to wait. I did not like to take notes in front of others.

Roger had found some mixed nuts. He brought me my drink and sat down across from me. He threw a large handful of nuts into his mouth.

"The record is over," I said.

"Do you want me to change it for you?"

"Yes please. I think Dvořák would be good."

Roger got up again, took the record off the phonograph, placing it on the sofa, and flipped through the shelf of records.

"Is this alphabetized? Where is it?"

"It's by the year of recording. The Dvořák I want to hear is 1937."

Roger put the record on and started back to his chair.

"Roger," I said faintly.

"Yes?"

"Roger, please put the other record back in its sleeve. It's there on the top shelf."

Roger went back and replaced the *Moonlight Sonata* in its sleeve, then sat down with his drink.

"I bet you wonder why I'm here."

"Why are you here?"

"Anne is on tour, and the kids are with her parents. I'm a free man tonight. Hope you don't mind me coming so late, but you were up anyway."

"What time is it?"

"It's three."

"In the morning?"

"Yes, of course it's morning! It's dark out, see?"

The time helped me get my bearings and I looked about me. I took a sip of my drink and felt refreshed. Roger was saying things to me, but I was thinking about my grandfather's music collection, which was mine now. He had promised to bequeath it to me in his will, and I was surprised on his death that he had actually remembered. He had been struck by my fascination with his large collection of records when I was still young. I was seven or eight years old, when one day he came upon me one day flipping methodically through the records and reading each title.

"Would you like to hear one?" He had asked. He looked amused. I was flattered that he was taking a personal interest in me. Even as small children, my cousins and I were aware that he was a great thinker—an influential man. We did not expect grandfatherly treatment from such a distinguished figure, and our mothers had taught us that we should feel honored to know him and that he was more important than the president of the United States. I took my charge seriously and always tried my utmost to fade into the background when he was in the room. I did not want to disgrace myself by impeding the progress of his thinking for I felt that the weight of the world was on his shoulders. No doubt he had addressed me before this occasion, but it was at that moment that I felt he perceived me as a fully realized human and not simply an appendage of my mother. I knew it was so when he spoke.

"Yes," I replied. "I would like to hear this one."

"That's an opera," he said. "Do you want to hear an opera?"

"Yes, I do," I said. "I want to hear 'Boris Godunov.'"

He laughed, either at the precocity of the request or my childish pronunciation of the word 'Godunov.' "Well, let's hear it then," he said. "What you need to understand with operas," he went on, "is that they are recorded on many records. When you take each record out of its jacket, you must look at the little number in the middle so you know what order to play them in. Do you understand, Daniel?"

"I understand."

"*Boris Godunov* has four records, that means eight sides. On this record player we can stack up all four records in order, one, two, three, four, don't forget that they are backwards, because the bottom one will drop first, like this. Then you just switch it on. Why don't you press the switch?"

I pressed the switch. The first record dropped and the opera began. I stood absolutely still, listening and watching the record spin round and round, the light reflected on its satiny, lined surface. My grandfather stood with me. I knew he was watching me. He was wearing his weekend clothes, dark brown corduroy pants, and a tan sweater. His corduroy pants always seemed to collect smells. I had always used those smells to invent stories of what he did with his days. That day his pants smelled faintly of steak and boiled eggs. Also, tobacco. He was a great thinker, but he also enjoyed a well-cooked meal. This endeared him to me greatly.

"Do you like it?" he had asked.

"Yes."

"Do you like to hear records?"

"Yes."

"One day, when I'm gone, I'll leave my record collection to you. I have been building this collection since I was a teenager and it is very precious to me. I think you might be the one to take care of it properly. What do you think?"

"Yes, I would like it. Thank you, Grandfather."

He smiled at me and winked, then wandered from the room. I sat next to the phonograph until each record had dropped and then I got up and carefully turned them all over to hear the second side. The auditory impact of the records on my child's ears fused inextricably with the honor that my grandfather had bestowed on me that day. I knew it then and I have never forgotten it.

Feeling refreshed, I got up and walked around the room and then looked at my desk. Roger was talking about a woman he had met at an art gallery with whom he had enjoyed a tryst earlier in the evening. I looked at my desk carefully and saw again the flyer for Dr. Antoinette Garner's lecture on prison writing.

"Roger?" I said.

"Yes?"

"I need to go to this lecture, but I'm afraid it will be hard for me to make sense of it. There are too many factors involved. If you came with me it would be easier."

"What is it?"

I showed him the flyer.

"You're going to a lecture on prison writing?" Roger sounded surprised.

"This woman, this is the confusing part, you see. This woman, who is giving the lecture, she is the head curator for the Schiffley House Archives. I met her when I went to Philadelphia."

"Oh, that's the connection. I knew your were planning to go to Schiffley House, but I didn't realize you had had a chance to speak with the head curator. I see. But then what's this about prison writing?"

"I don't know. I sort of know. I took notes, at the library today." I pointed vaguely toward my desk.

"And?"

"She wrote her dissertation on this subject. But I don't understand how she ended up at Schiffley House."

"That's interesting."

"She's very tall and beautiful. Also, she's black."

"More and more interesting. I think I just might have to join you."

"Would you? I just don't think I can go on my own."

"Let's do it! It's tomorrow?"

"Yes. But Roger, one other thing."

"What?"

"I also invited Uncle Ned."

"Oh, God, why did you do that? Is he still off the wagon?"

"Do you have to call it that?"

"I'm sorry, I know how you feel."

"It's just such unsavory rhetoric."

"I know, I know. I know how you feel. I'm sorry. It's just last time I saw Ned, he was, I mean, you know how it was... at your mother's Christmas party."

"I know. I know he can be very extreme. He was very drunk that night. But he's been much better lately, and my mother has asked me to take him to interesting events that don't involve alcohol, so I promised her. She worries about him so much."

"It's fine. I'm sure there won't be drinks there. As long as he doesn't pass a bar on the way!"

Roger always seemed to find drunks such as my Uncle Ned both repulsive and amusing. He was chuckling now, no doubt over some gaffe Ned had made after too many glasses of Christmas punch. Ned was badly off, but he had always been so. I thought of drunkenness as part of his personality. It was part of who he was and it seemed almost unnatural when that part of his personality was removed and replaced by the slogans, the meetings and the support groups. It lobotomized him and reduced him to something less than himself.

Roger had nodded off in his chair. Gradually the dawn light began to creep in through the windowpanes. Even in the dimmest early morning the windows became bright and glistening as the sun hit the fine networks of frost that spanned each pinkly glowing pane. In that moment, seated in my armchair, an empty glass resting in my hand, I suddenly realized what it was that I needed to do. It was time to find Grand Jane's table and bring it back into the family by whatever means necessary. In the morning I would call my mother and start making inquiries. I turned off the phonograph and switched off the lights. Then I went to the other room and lay down on my bed. My limbs were exhausted and there was much to do that afternoon. I slept.

10

Ned and I met Roger at the lecture hall. The event was scheduled at a nearby university campus in a large, unprepossessing science classroom with rows of gray desks attached in graduated semi-circles. The turnout was modest, perhaps about thirty-five people in all, most of whom seemed to know each other. We sat aloof as the other members of the audience greeted one another and Antoinette, who seemed to know them all as well. Antoinette wore a short-sleeved navy blue woolen dress over a white turtleneck and brown leather boots, almost butterscotch in color. Her costume was simple, but elegant, and she looked even more striking than I had remembered. Roger noticed her instantly and followed her with his eyes as she moved about at the front of the room. Ned seemed unfocused and slightly confused at first, but the topic was an interesting one, and he slowly cheered up as the talk progressed.

Antoinette's presentation was a literary analysis of the

writings that she had collected while doing her research for her thesis. In her introduction, she explained that because her dissertation had examined the sociological aspect of prison writing programs, she had not had the opportunity to discuss the actual writing of the prisoners she interviewed. The writing itself deserved more attention, she explained, and this presentation was the beginning of an analysis of that work, and would become an introduction to a forthcoming anthology of the writings discussed. It was clear that the other members of the audience were quite familiar with Antoinette's previous work. Some of those present may even have been former interviewees and inmates, as their demeanor seemed of a rougher type than that of the graduate students and professors in the room.

After forty-five minutes the lecture was completed, and Antoinette began to take questions. Though she was in a surrounding of familiar faces and was comfortable with the material she discussed, there was still an air of distance and coldness about her. Her hair was fastened tightly in a bun, giving her face a more severe look. We were sitting apart from the rest of the audience and I kept wondering if she noticed us. Once or twice she seemed to glance our way, and I thought she might have recognized me, but perhaps her eye was caught by Uncle Ned's red velvet smoking jacket, his 'security blanket' as he called it. Ned always found it difficult to leave the house wearing ordinary street clothing when he was not drinking; he said it made it easier for him to resist temptation if he wore clothing that made him feel 'splendid.'

The question-and-answer period proceeded monotonously until I noticed that Ned was getting a little agitated. Suddenly, to my horror, he raised his hand and kept it in the air until he was sure that Antoinette had seen it. A few moments later, when she had finished answering a question, she turned to him and gave him an expectant look.

"Yes?" she asked.

"Dr. Garner. Thank you very much for a terrifically informative lecture."

"You are quite welcome." Antoinette smiled coolly.

"Really, I really enjoyed it, thank you so much. Gosh, so interesting. Looking forward to the anthology."

"Thank you."

"My question is about the Schiffley archive."

Antoinette looked annoyed. Ned held up the flyer giving details about the talk that had been available outside the lecture hall.

"I see from this flyer, and I understand from my nephew here," he waved the flyer in my direction, "that you are the head archivist for Schiffley House." It was at this point that Antoinette noticed me for the first time. I sank nervously into the coat that I had kept draped about my shoulders.

"Yes, that is correct."

"My question is, well, goodness. I have so many questions! Our family history goes way back with the Schiffleys, but leaving that aside I just want to say how fascinated I am. I mean, what's the connection? This lecture, so insightful, your analysis, and then oversight of such a notorious archive—fascinating."

I felt humiliated. I should never have listened to my mother. Uncle Ned is bound to ruin everything if given the opportunity. It doesn't matter if there's drink involved. I felt everyone's eyes on us, as some groups in the audience began to whisper.

Antoinette fixed Ned with an expressionless gaze and replied, "I'm not sure if I know what your question is."

Suddenly Roger was speaking. "I believe what my friend is asking is a question about the overall, the framing trajectory of your—the theoretical concerns in your work." Roger was leaning forward, a charming smile on his face. He had an enviable way of making words and phrases sound natural and conversational that would be awkward or pedantic coming from a less eloquent speaker. "The archives of a prominent American family, the writings of prison inmates, there is doubtless a connection here that undergirds the big questions of your work."

Ned smiled. Roger was not rephrasing his question and he knew this. Despite the fact that he could at times like these appear to be 'not all there,' he was a brilliant man in his own way, and his ability to follow complex arguments was what had taken him so far in his study of classical philosophy. He smiled, and this was because he was always entertained by academic fencing and he knew that Roger's question, more so than his own, would take the conversation into an area of theoretical discomfort for everyone. Roger, of course, was oblivious to this. Roger himself did not entirely understand what he had just said, and was only attempting to defuse an embarrassing Ned situation while taking advantage of the opportunity to get the attention of an attractive woman.

I wanted nothing more than to slink away and retreat to my apartment to reflect upon Antoinette's presentation. I wondered the same thing Ned did, but to me it was a puzzle that needed to be deciphered. Asking the question directly seemed a method bound to fail and something that would simply throw the whole issue into a greater state of confusion. I was sure Antoinette would be even more displeased now. To my surprise, however, her features softened into a slight smile.

"Thank you for asking that question. It's critical to the way I think about both of my spheres of interest. We're running out of time right now, so let me just say briefly that my connection to both subjects is personal, but in terms of theoretical questions, both present us with very rich material on citizenship, nationalism and freedom."

At this point the Chair of the Department of Criminology, who had been poised to spring out of his chair when Ned started to ask his question, rushed up to the podium and starting clapping vigorously. He thanked Antoinette and the audience and remarked that it had been a successful event. He seemed to be eager to end it, and was in the process of ushering Antoinette out of the room when she stopped and turned to look toward us. Brushing aside a number of breathless graduate students, she walked up the steps toward our party. I felt uneasy. This was not the meeting I had had in mind. When she reached us, she put out her hand to greet me.

"I did not expect to see you here," she said.

"I happened to see an announcement," I responded. "I

have read your article, and have been writing you a letter on the topic."

Antoinette looked at Roger and Ned expectantly. "And this is my friend Roger Pencil. And my Uncle Ned," I added.

"Pleased to meet you both."

Ned and Roger both began talking at once, praising her lecture and asking questions. Roger seemed suddenly to know a great deal about prison literature. He peppered his questions with references to Gramsci and when Antoinette spoke, he cocked his head to one side and listened reverently. With his rakish three-piece tweed suit and brown leather spectator shoes, one had to admit he looked dashing. Soon Ned drifted over to me, sensing himself cut out of the conversation.

"I believe Dr. Garner's hosts are waiting for her," I interjected, hoping to avoid further conversation that would disrupt my interactions with Antoinette.

"Oh yes," she smiled. "I should go to the reception. But it would be nice to finish this conversation," she added.

"Well perhaps you could join us for dinner," suggested Roger eagerly. "Lots of great places around here."

"Yes, yes," added Ned. "We really have to continue this conversation. So much to ask about the Schiffleys and Dad, and you know, these prison things. Wow, that research, quite something! Fascinating, really. I really mean that." Ned beamed. He loved to talk to other intellectuals, though the conversations usually ended badly.

"Well, I think I could make time for dinner," said Antoinette, choosing her words carefully. I was confused by the relative warmth in her tone when she said this, and I felt fairly convinced that it was not directed toward me, and certainly not toward Ned. Roger must be working his magic again; I was taken aback that a scholar as imposing as Antoinette could be so quickly seduced.

Antoinette invited us to the reception hosted by the Department of Criminology, and we helped ourselves to some cheese and crackers and stayed in the corner of the room away from the tight-knit circle of scholars in attendance. Ned moved uneasily from one foot to the other, brushing the back of his velvet jacket against the patterned stucco of the walls of the Criminology lounge. Wine and beer were being served, and he did not venture to the part of the room where these were laid out along with the cheese and crackers. Instead I brought him some food on a small paper plate.

"Terrible booze. Look." Ned blinked rapidly and pointed in what he thought was a subtle fashion toward the wine and beer. "These things, always low budget." This was a ritual Ned went through in order to resist temptation. He rejected the worn out phrases that are taught in rehabilitation programs in favor of a method he had developed that consisted of distancing himself from alcoholic beverages through actual physical distance and snobbery. This worked well enough unless he found himself in a small space with high quality liquors.

After about an hour, the reception had reached its crescendo and the graduate students, who appeared slightly tipsy, began to leave, their pockets suspiciously bulging with shapes that might have been wedges of Brie wrapped in white paper napkins. Ned was making an argument to Roger that Virgil had been an author of rare comic genius, and I was turning over in my mind a strategy whereby we might go out to dinner with Antoinette and without Ned, or, failing that, find our way to a restaurant that did not serve alcohol, for I had promised my mother that I would take him out for activities that would distract him from his vice. I had narrowed down our choices for dining to three, each within a ten minute walk of the campus: a Chinese restaurant that had recently lost its liquor license for serving alcohol to college students, a vegetarian restaurant with no liquor, and a café that was open late and had a reasonable menu of soups and sandwiches.

Just then one of the young men with cheeses stowed in his jacket pockets approached me, for I was standing alone, slightly apart from Ned and Roger.

"Hey," said the young man. "Are you in the Department?"

"No," I replied nervously, suddenly wondering if the reception had not been open after all, although Antoinette had invited us.

"Oh wow, so you just came to see Dr. Garner, then, huh?"

"Yes, that's correct."

He introduced himself and held out his hand. I shook it.

"Daniel," I said.

"So what brings you here? Do you work on prison lit?"

"No, no. Actually, we are more familiar with Dr. Garner's work as an archivist for the Schiffley House."

"Oh, right. You guys asked those questions at the end."

"Yes, they did."

"Amazing, amazing stuff. Dr. Garner is such an amazing scholar. And human being, too, right? I mean, all that stuff with her uncle. Wow."

"Her uncle?"

"Oh, no. Don't tell me you don't know that whole story! Just incredible. Of course that's how she got into prison writing."

"No....no, I am afraid I don't know what you're talking about."

The young man was about to launch into his story when he saw that Antoinette was approaching us. He quickly changed the topic.

"So are you a researcher, or...?"

"In a manner of speaking. Yes. I'm working on some research."

"Are you ready for dinner?" Antoinette interrupted.

"Yes, yes, if you're ready to go." I hastily separated myself from the student and signaled to Roger and Ned.

"Now I've thought of three places we might go," I began.

"Oh, but that won't be necessary," said Antoinette firmly. "Whenever I'm here I insist on going to the Swabian Soup Kitchen on Pinecone. It has been my habit these ten years since I started to come up for conferences and research. I cannot leave the city without eating there, and this is my last night. You don't mind, do you?" Her question came in the tone of a command, and the three of us found ourselves shaking our heads vigorously.

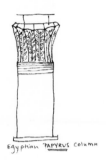

Egyptian "PAPYRUS Column"

11

When I look back at the evening, it seems clear that it was at this point that things began to go awry. Antoinette's choice of restaurant, coupled with the revelation that she might have been married put me in a discomfited state. On top of this, there had been her lecture, a theoretically complicated presentation on a topic about which I knew little and had considered less. And then there was Roger's apparent interest in Antoinette, and my awkward custodial position vis-à-vis Ned.

Later that night, seated at my desk, I attempted to gather my thoughts and make sense of the evening by writing out my reflections in a notebook. By this point in my reflections, I had noted down the main arguments from Antoinette's lecture, I had sketched an outline of the conversations between the lecture and the dinner, I had listed the items on the menu at the Swabian Kitchen, and what dishes each of us had chosen and I had diagrammed the dinner table conversation. But no amount of categorizing and systematizing seemed to allay the unpleasant feeling at the pit of my stomach.

I rose from my desk, my nerves somewhat steadied by the note taking. Pouring myself a glass of port wine, I walked over to my record collection. The turntable had stopped moving, and I pulled aside the needle to lift the record off the phonograph and replace it in its sleeve. I checked the needle on the record player for good measure. It still looked new, as I had replaced it only a few months before when I had had to get the record player repaired for the third time that year. It was difficult keeping such a delicate piece of machinery in good repair when there were so few people with expertise in the upkeep of phonographs nowadays. As I lifted the record off the spindle, I stopped for a moment. I thought I saw a small scratch illuminated by the nearby lamp onto the shining surface of the record, but I was mistaken. It seemed to be a hair. I wiped down the record and replaced it in its sleeve. I stopped for a moment to examine the edges of the sleeve, as I always worry about the wear and tear to the cardboard that is caused when one pulls the records on and off the shelves. It was in good enough condition, though my affection for that particular record was evidenced by the slight roughness at the corners. I pushed the record back into its place on the shelf and felt suddenly overwhelmed with a wave of sadness for the passage of time and the ultimate destructibility of my grandfather's record collection.

After a moment, I decided that trite though it might seem, my late-night musings should be accompanied by Chopin's nocturnes. New music and drink in place, I returned to my desk. Perhaps this wouldn't be such a hard night after all. I felt better already. I placed my palms on each side of my notebook and gazed at my account of the menu with great concentration. Swabian cuisine is heavy and tends to favor large quantities of meat and various starchy items such as spätzle. The restaurant where we dined, though traditional, made allowances for American tastes, serving smaller cuts of meat and offering more fresh vegetables than might be found in Germany. Though the menu included a number of wines and beers, no one ordered any liquor at the outset, so Ned was initially kept in check, though he did on several occasions ask if anyone wished to wash down their food with a tankard of ale.

Roger and I both firmly said no, and Antoinette had remarked that she did not like to drink alcohol with meat. This was a surprising assertion, and a lively conversation ensued in which, I believe, I managed to impress Antoinette to no small degree with my knowledge of pure and blended tastes. This conversation led to the topic of various cuisines of the world, and by the time that was exhausted, we had already begun our main courses. It was at this point that Ned began to ask Antoinette some pointed questions about her views on my grandfather and the Schiffleys.

"So, Dr. Garner—Antoinette, if I may—"

"Please."

"Antoinette. This has been a tremendous evening. Tremendous. And I'm sure you know what I'm going to ask. I'd like to pick up where we left off in the seminar, if I might. I mean, gosh. I'd really like to know more about your work, the prison stuff and then Schiffley, of course. I confess I am curious to know what you find defensible about the Schiffleys...."

Antoinette smiled stiffly and put down her fork. Under the table I began to twist my paper napkin, slowly shredding it to bits. Roger seemed unperturbed and picked up the topic.

"Yes, we were talking about your work but then we ran out of time! Tell us more—I think we're all curious. You said something about narratives of citizenship?"

Antoinette relaxed slightly and sat back in her chair.

"I think I mentioned that both of my professional interests had a personal component to them."

"Yes!" Ned interrupted. "Now how could that be? Tell us that story. Let's have it *ab initio*." He smiled happily as he tapped his forefinger rapidly on the edge of the table. I followed his gaze, which was fixed slightly above Antoinette's shoulder. He seemed to be staring at a young couple sitting in the corner sharing a bottle of wine; above their heads hung an old and faded print in the style of Breughel, depicting some hearty peasants seated at wooden plank tables swigging from earthenware jugs of ale.

Antoinette picked up her fork again and pushed at the edges of the pile of spätzle, tidying it up as though her fork were a tiny snowplow. She was silent for a moment.

"When I was a child, my Uncle Rex was falsely accused of a terrible crime," she began. "He was accused, tried, and sentenced to life in prison."

This was an unexpected turn for the conversation to take.

Everyone busied themselves with the food on their plates, afraid that any interruption would break the flow of her story.

"Uncle Rex's trial and subsequent imprisonment had a devastating effect on our family. My father became acutely depressed and for a time he was prescribed so much medication that he was no better than a vegetable. My mother had to work two jobs to support us. We all moved in together, with Rex's wife and children. After three years of living in cramped quarters with my father incapacitated, he happened to receive treatment from a brilliant psychologist at the University Hospital."

By now we had all forgotten our food. Antoinette put down her fork and folded her hands in her lap. Her body was perfectly still as she spoke.

"The psychologist, Dr. Ernst Brocken, perhaps you've heard his name?"

"Why yes—Brocken—didn't he write a very interesting book on grieving? I think I read excerpts somewhere," responded Ned hesitantly.

"Yes, that's right. His seminal work was *Broken Swallows*. My father's case is featured in that book. I won't go into the treatment he pursued, but one aspect was to encourage my father to visit his brother at least once a week in prison. He hadn't gone at all, you see. So his grief for his brother's situation resembled a state of mourning; in his mind, his brother was dead. Dr. Brocken wanted him to see that he was still alive.

"I was twelve years old when my father began his weekly visits to the prison to see Uncle Rex. Uncle Rex, contrary to his expectations, was thriving. He had become a community leader behind bars, a prayer leader and a mentor. My father was caged by his sorrow, and his brother, who was in prison, had found a new freedom. Most importantly, he had finished his high school education in those years since we had seen him, and had regularly enrolled in creative writing courses that were offered there, taught by local writers and some graduate students from the universities."

"And thus—we begin to see the connection with prison narratives! Bravo!" Ned was enthused. He slapped his hand on the table and chuckled.

"So what did he write? What was he writing, your Uncle Rex, in prison?" asked Roger, clearly riveted.

"Rex was not a particularly creative man. But he developed a good style and he wrote many things; the most important work he produced was a collection of short narratives of other prisoners. He gathered their stories, like an ethnography. I have devoted a chapter to this genre in my book, because it's an important genre of prison writing."

"And you quote your uncle?" Asked Roger.

"Yes, but I try to draw on a mix of authors."

"Amazing! I'd love to see how this connects to the Schiffleys. Don't tell me they were behind bars too, that would be too good to be true, eh, Daniel?" Ned tried to include me in his sentiment by patting me on the shoulder. I shrank in my seat.

"Ned, I don't believe the Schiffleys were ever incarcerated," I muttered back between clenched teeth. I couldn't believe he was breaking the spell of this magical moment with his inane observations.

Antoinette stared at Ned through narrowed eyes.

"That is correct, the Schiffleys were never incarcerated." She paused. "The Schiffleys are connected to this story, however. That is why I am relating it to you."

"Those were the days when I met Larry Schiffley. And I did meet him in the prison, but he was not a prisoner. He came regularly to visit a prisoner, a former groundskeeper of his who had also been charged with murder, unjustly, Mr. Schiffley believed. Larry Schiffley fought that injustice for ten years until the man finally won an acquittal."

"Good God! Unbelievable! Daniel, you have to write all this down, it's going to be great for your research."

"It's on technology, Ned. I'm looking at the technology angle. I don't think so," I hissed.

"I am not ashamed to have these facts recorded," said Antoinette in a steady tone. "It was at this time that I became acquainted with Mr. Schiffley, and it offered me a special insight into his character. An insight that showed me a man of irreproachable character, of genuine kindness, of sterling values...." Her voice began to quaver as she looked down at her half-eaten plate of sausages and spätzle.

"Sterling values? Irreproachable character?" Ned could not contain himself. "The man who, single-handedly—no, with the help of his brother—(can you say 'double-handedly', I wonder?)—the man who—the Schiffleys who stole my father's patents and tried to destroy American foreign policy! Are we talking about the same Schiffleys—"

Ned was interrupted by the sound of Antoinette slamming her clenched fist on the table. The silverware clattered against the china, and my glass of water nearly tipped over. We all sat quietly, unsure what to do next.

Roger broke the silence. He leaned forward and spoke to Antoinette in a soft and confidential tone. "This is such an interesting story and your perspective is a revelation. I think that's what Ned means—we want to hear more! We've never heard this side of the story. Isn't that right, Daniel? Ned?"

Ned looked like he was going to have another outburst, but I interjected quickly. "Yes, yes, that's how we feel. We've been told another story all our lives, people in our family have, and we'd like to hear your perspective. Thank you for sharing it with us. We are honored."

Ned looked around the table, and then, crumpling up his napkin in his hand beside his plate, he answered carefully, "Yes, yes, please. Apologies, please go on."

"I think I would like a drink after all," said Antoinette, her voice low and tense.

I looked anxiously at Roger, hoping he would know what to do. The situation was beyond me. Roger did not meet my gaze; he had already hailed the waitress. He was in the process of ordering a bottle of wine.

"Or did you want beer?" He turned to Antoinette.

"Wine will be fine, thank you."

Nothing could have been worse. Ned's eyes darted around the table as the waitress uncorked the bottle and offered a sip to Roger to taste. She had brought four glasses.

Roger was talking to Antoinette. "I think you're going to like this if you like Rieslings. It's not too sweet; it has a light flavor...do you like Rieslings?"

Antoinette nodded, avoiding eye contact with anyone. It may have been the case that she was close to tears, but it was difficult to tell.

As the waitress handed a glass to Ned, I glanced fearfully at Roger. I raised my eyebrows in alarm. Roger squinted and shook his head slightly. I could see that he was going to be no help.

"Ned, if you don't want any, I'm sure one of us can drink yours," I suggested hesitantly. "I don't think it's a particularly good wine," I whispered as an afterthought, hoping to appeal to his snobbery.

But physical proximity had already been breached, and Ned was sniffing the glass with a quizzical look on his face. He tasted it. "I think it's rather nice, Daniel. Don't you like it? I think Roger has made quite a nice choice. You can't really get top drawer at places like this, you know." Another sip. "Yes, it's not too sweet, you were right, Roger. Daniel, why don't you try it?" A larger sip.

I sighed with resignation and took a sip as well. It was rather nice. I felt myself relaxing slightly and drank some more. It was not too sweet. I took out a small notebook and made a note of the name of the wine and my immediate reactions to it. Roger was still speaking to Antoinette quietly. She seemed to be relaxing and I thought I even heard her manage something close to a giggle while I was jotting down my notes.

When I looked up, the waitress was pouring more wine into all of our glasses.

"Thanks," said Ned. "It's a lovely wine. To Swabia!" He raised his glass cheerfully. We all toasted Swabia, and then we toasted some of the famous Swabians who had been listed on the back of the menu.

"To Albert Einstein!" toasted Ned.

Everyone thought for a moment. "To Hegel!" said Roger. "To Hermann Hesse!" I was thankful I had read the menu so carefully. "To Heidegger!" Antoinette giggled more audibly this time, and turned and smiled at Roger, perhaps thankful that he had managed to alleviate the mood with this bottle of wine. We started to discuss Heidegger for a while, and somehow another bottle of wine materialized on the table. Ned quoted Horace for us to illustrate some point about German philosophers, or perhaps about wine. His color had deepened, as it does, to a light magenta. The dinner plates had been cleared away and the dessert menus had been lying on the table ignored for some time. When Roger and Antoinette started off on a tangent, I began to study the dessert menu carefully. The meal had been characteristically heavy, and I was quite full, but I wanted to make sure that there wasn't anything unusual or exceptional that I might be missing. At this point, Ned leaned close to me.

"Have I done something...very wrong?" he asked, with an impish sort of smile.

"No—what—?" I wasn't sure how to answer, as it was not clear to which action the question referred.

"I mean, before!" He clasped my shoulder warmly in his by now sweaty palm. "I think I may have spoken out of turn a bit." He smiled conspiratorially at me. "Threw her for a bit of a loop!" he said in a stage whisper and rolled his eyes in Antoinette's direction. Thankfully, Antoinette did not seem to hear him.

"I think," I began, not sure how to express this to Ned in his present state, "I think that we must keep our feelings and prejudices..."

"Prejudices!" Ned exclaimed loudly. Antoinette and Roger looked over at us. I laughed heartily to make it seem as though Ned had told me a joke to which 'prejudices' was the punch line. It seemed to do the trick and they turned back to their conversation.

"We must keep our family feelings to ourselves," I spoke slowly and cautiously, "because we want to know the story she is telling, and we shouldn't interrupt her when she is speaking."

"Ah. I see. I see what you mean. You've always been very good at subtle, Daniel. Very good at subtle. Remember—no, you wouldn't—you were a baby—but remember the story about when you were a baby, and there was that time that you wanted something but no one knew what it was?"

"Yes, Ned, I have heard that story. Mother tells it often."

"Oh, yes, she would. It was quite something, you know. And there you were in your highchair. You learn so much about a person at that age, when you wouldn't think they had any personality to speak of!" Ned chortled at his own joke and drank the rest of his glass of wine in a single swig.

"Shall we get dessert?" I raised my voice and pointedly addressed Roger and Antoinette, who seemed to have gotten quite cozy at their end of the table.

"Oh, certainly, they have some excellent puddings here," said Antoinette gesturing absentmindedly at the menu.

"And if we could, my dear lady," interjected Ned, turning to Antoinette, "Perhaps nothing would sweeten our palates more successfully than a return to your fascinating narration of earlier? I'm afraid this wine has proved rather a distraction to us!" He laughed boisterously and waved his hand toward the wine in a wide arc, a gesture which narrowly missed knocking my empty wine glass and some of the water glasses off the table.

This remark froze me with terror. It had already been bad enough without the wine, but Ned was now clearly intoxicated and his behavior was unlikely to improve. I looked at Roger beseechingly. He could see that the situation was likely to deteriorate. Antoinette was becoming emotional again. There was a distant look in her eyes.

"I believe it is rather late," she said in a slow and deliberate tone. "I should be getting back to my hotel."

"But what a cliffhanger!" Ned was greatly amused and clearly did not see that he had yet again ruined the mood.

"Why don't I walk you back to your hotel?" Roger asked Antoinette in a soothing tone. "Daniel, you can help Ned get home."

"Help Ned! Old Uncle Ned! Well, I don't think I'm so old that I can't make it home on my own!" Ned's voice was getting louder and the veins on his neck bulged out above his shirt collar. "I dare say I can make my own way home..." He stood up and swayed slightly, grabbing hold of my arm. He put out his other hand to steady himself on the table and grabbed at the table cloth, knocking over his glass of wine with a clink. "I dare say..." Ned looked around him vacantly. I handed him his coat and hat.

"Let me take you home, Uncle Ned. Here."

"But what about our story! Wonderful woman! Isn't she a wonderful woman? So...Egyptian, regal. Don't you think she's regal, Daniel? Like Cleopatra, no other. I pronounce you Queen of the Nile," he cried out thunderously, turning to face Antoinette, his coat half on, and his hat perched crookedly on his head. "Queen of the Nile!"

Antoinette gave him an icy stare. "I'm ready." She turned to Roger, who was buttoning up his coat. He saw that the matter was now urgent.

"Well, see you later, Daniel, Ned. It's been an interesting evening." He smiled charmingly to both of us and rushed out of the restaurant after Antoinette's swiftly retreating figure.

"Daniel? Dan? Have I done something wrong again? Danny Boy..." Ned went swiftly from remorseful to cheerful, as he began to whistle the tune to "Danny Boy," a practice he had initiated when I was a child.

"Let's go, Ned." I took him firmly by the arm and led him out of the restaurant, as he attempted to linger, thanking the waitresses, the hostess and the bartender. For each of these, he would lift his hat and say a random phrase in German that had occurred to him at that instant. I tugged at his sleeve and finally got him out the door.

The air was cold and it seemed to dampen Ned's spirits somewhat. Ned's apartment was a brisk fifteen-minute walk away, and I got him there as fast as I could, pulling him along and trying to avoid other pedestrians on the street, whom he would invariably address in German if we passed too closely. Periodically he would stop, throw his hands in the air and cry out into the night, "Queen of Denial!" And then, laughing uproariously, he would slap me on the back. After getting him home and into his pajamas, I made him a cup of coffee and gave him some aspirin, as my mother always did when he was drunk. He seemed somewhat calmed and promised me he would go directly to bed.

"You won't go out again tonight, will you, Uncle Ned?"

"Who me? Oh no, oh no. Your Uncle Ned is old, old. I leave the carousing to you young people, Daniel, Danny."

"I think I will turn in myself, actually."

"But you are young!" Ned waved his hand around in the air lazily, to indicate something to do with youth. "You are young—dance! Drink! Enjoy the company of attractive young ladies!" He gestured vaguely to indicate young ladies.

"Not tonight, Uncle Ned, I have some writing to do." I smiled at the thought of myself engaging in the sorts of activities that Ned must imagine as the dalliances of young people. "I'll take your leave now. You will go to sleep, then?"

"To sleep... to sleep, perchance to dream...." Ned looked abstracted. "There has been so much talk of German tonight,

I must listen to a German composer." He got up and wandered absentmindedly over to his record player. "What do you say, Daniel? *Kindertotenlieder* fit the mood?" He laughed knowingly.

"Certainly, Ned, but perhaps something on the lighter side."

"The lighter side of the Germans? I think not, young man, I think not." He carefully put a record onto the record player. As the music began to play, he turned unsteadily and roughly held onto the table that held the phonograph, causing the needle to skip a couple of times. He waved his arm in the air. "Now be gone, young man, leave an old man to his contemplations of dead children." He chuckled to himself and then lost his train of thought, staring at me vacantly for a moment. "Good night, young man, and pleasant dreams. 'Twas a wonderful evening indeed."

"Good night, Uncle Ned."

I took my leave.

It had been an extraordinarily difficult and over-stimulating day. Not only had the lecture and dinner proved troublesome, but I had also initiated my search for the fruit table by calling my mother, who had promised to look into it. I continued to have trouble recording my thoughts. I thought to play an opera but then decided against it. My senses felt fragile and the intensity of opera would have done little to soothe them. I stood for some time in front of my shelves of records and mused over what might be an appropriate choice. I finally selected the Brandenburg Concertos as conducted by Harnoncourt, which proved altogether wrong; ten minutes in, I threw down my pen and hurried back over to the phonograph to remove the record as quickly as possible. I then selected a record of the Pablo Casals Bach cello suites with some misgivings. The task had inspired me with a sense of urgency for I felt I needed to fill the room with sound such that my mental state would be tamed, calmed and contained. Only then could I record my impressions of the day by means of pen and paper. Without the right music, the size and chaotic constitution of my thoughts were rendered utterly unmanageable. I needed the music to help order my thoughts.

This time I was encouraged to find a calm descending about the room, and the strains of the cello, like some sorcerer's wand, induced a trancelike state in my thoughts, a tangle of rioting serpents, and slowly pushed them to reenter their container and repose there in semi-somnolence.

12

Some months after the ill-fated dinner at the Swabian restaurant, I was finishing an indulgent breakfast of orange juice, hot coffee and two croissants, when I received a telephone call from my mother.

"You did not call," she said, in response to my greeting.

I was perturbed. "Was I supposed to?"

"I had sent a message for you to call, but you didn't."

"You sent a message?"

"Yes, from the computer, but you didn't respond, even though you promised you would."

I realized then that my mother must have sent me a message via electronic mail. A few months before, we had both agreed to succumb to the widespread pressure brought to bear by friends and family to set up email accounts so that we would be more easily reached. Though we had both protested that we were just as easy to find as we had ever been, we finally agreed to take the plunge. We had made a pact to start off with a trial period, during which we would only send electronic messages to one another. This way we could test the medium without opening the floodgates to others, thereby making it impossible to retreat to our original position if we decided to discontinue the practice. We had also agreed to make paper copies of our emails to one another to be kept in our files for archival purposes, should the need arise at some later date.

In my distaste for electronic mail, I was proving even more recalcitrant than my mother. I had promised to check my messages every other day, but I realized when she called that I had not checked them for four, or maybe even five, days. For the purposes of connecting to the internet, I had purchased a small, used laptop computer, but had nowhere to put it. It wouldn't have done to disrupt the composition of my desk by placing it there, so I had ended up storing it in the hallway linen closet among the sheets. Because of this, it only occurred to me to check my messages when I had call to change my bed linens or remove a fresh towel for the bath, occasions that arose usually no more than once a week. At times, the computer would accidentally get completely covered by a pile of laundered sheets, and then it might be more than a week before I came upon it again. But it must also be said that my poor record in checking for messages could be traced to the fact that if I did not respond, my mother would invariably call, sometimes within hours, and relay the same message over the telephone. And so it had occurred on this day, when she called and expressed her displeasure at my tardy response.

"What did you wish to tell me, when you wrote?" I asked, hoping to change the subject. I could hear a great clatter of pots in the background and I imagined my mother engaging in some kitchen reorganization project while simultaneously calling me on the phone. She loathed idleness and had had a phone with an extra long cord installed in the kitchen so that she could engage in useful tasks while discussing urgent matters on the phone.

"It was days ago, and I wanted to tell you something very interesting and to ask your advice about how to pursue it, but you didn't respond, so I've had to do it all myself. I really do wish you'd check your emails more often. It's what we said we'd do."

"I'm very sorry, Mother," I said. "I just forget to check because the computer is in the linen closet."

"Well why don't you take it out then, or leave yourself a reminder on the icebox? If you don't start responding, I will have to find someone else to exchange messages with, and that would be so boring."

"But I thought that was the goal, ultimately? That we would correspond with other people who used email regularly?"

"Yes, perhaps you are right. One just worries about getting it wrong."

"I'm sure you will do well," I assured her. "But what is it you wanted to tell me?"

"Oh, yes, it's the table you were asking about, the fruit table in Grandfather's house that turned out really to belong to

Grand Jane."

My interest was piqued. I sat down at my desk and picked up a pen and paper in preparation for any notes I might need to take. "Yes, tell me."

"Well, I ran into our lawyer, Bente Jorgenson, during the intermission of a new production of *Blithe Spirits* at the Playhouse that I went to with Aunt Sooly. Not very well done, I'm afraid. The sets were all wrong and you should have heard the lead actor's accent. It was atrocious! He was trying to sound British, but his accent kept coming all to pieces. Your father would have died. Anyway, I saw Bente during the intermission and she asked after you, and then it occurred to me to ask her about it, because her father, who is now retired, was the executor of the will and worked for Grandfather and Grand Jane for many, many years. Bente said she would look in their files to see who Grand Jane's heirs were, apart from us, of course."

"Yes?"

"And she called me the next day and said she had found a list, and said she would give me the name of the nephew who received the table, but that I mustn't tell anyone." She had clearly warmed to her subject, as the clanging of pots had ceased. I imagined her sitting at her modestly sized table in the buttery yellow kitchen, the morning sun streaming through the windows over the sink. Or perhaps not, as it was cloudy out and it might be already raining there.

"Oh, wonderful!" I was thrilled, but then worried. "That's not a violation of confidentiality, or anything like that?"

"She said it was a gray area, but since I had told her how

anxious you were to learn more about the table, she said of course she would tell me, because her father, who is dead now, had always been so fond of you and delighted by your many interests, and I do remember once he brought you some figurines from England for your china collection."

"Oh, how kind of her. This is very exciting news, Mother."

"You will have to write her a thank you note, because I do think it may be that she was not supposed to share this information. Should I give you her address?"

"Of course I will write, right away. But you can give me the address later. First tell me about this nephew."

"Yes, yes, so his name is James De Lourgnier."

"How is that spelled?" I asked, my pen stopping short at the last name.

"Big D, little e, space, big L, o-u-r-g-n-i-e-r."

"That sounds French," I said, puzzled.

"Yes, it does, I am not sure where the name comes from. Not from Grand Jane's family, clearly. It must be from the other side."

"Did you get any more information about this man? Any addresses?"

"Bente did have an address, but it was from years ago. Somewhere in California, I think. That's why I wanted you to call me, so we could decide how to proceed. But you didn't call, so I called Aunt Sooly to see what she thought, because she is really so resourceful. And she had the wonderful idea that I could call that detective she had hired a few years ago to follow Uncle Frank when he she thought he was running around with the woman from the golf club. What's her name, that tennis instructor with red hair who ended up marrying Dale Wingback and then they moved to Gstaad."

"Oh, brilliant! So you called him?"

"Yes, I did. He was a lovely man with a very full dark beard, and the thickest glasses you've ever seen, and he found information about James De Lourgnier right away. I told him it was absolutely like magic, and he was a dear. He said, 'It was nothing you couldn't have done yourself by looking at the internet,' and I said, 'That certainly is something I could not have done for myself!' He laughed and tried not to charge me anything for it, but I insisted he must be compensated because it was absolutely brilliant what he found."

"And what did he find? Where is he? Who is this James De Lourgnier?" I said, pronouncing the last name slowly and carefully. "I wonder if he pronounces it in the French way, or if it's Americanized."

"I really don't know, dear. But it seems he is a professor at the University of Mississippi in Oxford, of all places. He is a professor of art history. The detective printed out a copy of his information on the internet. He looks perfectly nice and is probably about your age, or maybe a little bit older? It looks like he is balding. It says he's written all sorts of books and articles, so he must be quite smart."

"Mississippi! That's very far. I've never been to the South. I wonder what made him choose to move there. Does that page give any indication of how to contact him?"

"Yes, there is a phone number for his department, and

also an email address."

"Tell me both," I sighed, eyeing the linen closet. "Who knows if his department will give me his personal phone number."

After I had thanked my mother profusely, I got off the phone and considered what my plan of attack should be. I felt exhilarated. It was difficult to compose myself adequately to make preparations for the steps I would need to take in light of this exciting new development. I decided to send an email message, and then follow up with a phone call to the department. Then I could ask them for a mailing address as well. If James would receive me, I would have to formulate a travel plan as well. I couldn't imagine how one traveled to Oxford, Mississippi, but I hoped I would be able to avoid going by air. My suitcase needed some repairs on the clasp, and I would have to get my woolen trousers pressed. What books should I bring? I began to make a list.

Part II : Quest

table leg
(detail)

13

For my trip to Oxford, I booked a sleeper compartment from Boston to Chicago, and another from Chicago to Memphis. By train, one could get no closer to Oxford than Memphis, some eighty or so miles to the northeast. To travel from Memphis to Oxford, I would have to hire a taxicab at considerable cost, an option that seemed better than the other possibilities, such as a bus, or a rental car. Though I am able to drive a car, and hold a license to operate a vehicle, I have always strongly preferred to avoid driving, unless it is for small errands when I am visiting my mother.

I had managed to reach James De Lourgnier via email message, and he warmly invited me to dinner at his home whenever I might come to town; but due to a busy schedule of academic conferences and speaking engagements, he was only able to suggest a few evenings in late October, a fortnight hence, from which to choose. I was very fortunate to find single sleeping compartments for each leg of my journey on such short notice.

I was not so convinced of my good fortune upon boarding the first train, however. The unappealing smells of the Amtrak sleeper carriage, the cramped space, the ill-fitting bed linens and the stained floors were all features of the journey for which I was unprepared. I had always imagined overnight train travel would conform to descriptions I had read in novels and scenes in films, such as the compartment occupied by Cary Grant and Eva Marie Saint in *North by Northwest*. I confess that some of my expectations had been unreasonable, and were perhaps products of an overactive imagination, but despite the absence of a flowered carpet and matching drapes, perhaps a single rose in a vase on the table alongside the window, a modicum of attention to aesthetic details would have gone a long way toward allaying my fears of possible insect infestations, or larger human intruders in the dead of night. I felt unsure about the security of the lock on the door, and wondered if the window could be opened from the outside.

By suppertime, we had reached Albany. As I turned my steps toward the dining car, my heart sank as I observed along the hallway the stained carpet from which wafted the distinctive stench of disinfectant mingled with an array of other odors it had failed to mask. I already suspected that the linen tablecloths, the hanging lamps and the mysterious well-dressed strangers would fail to materialize. But it would have been impossible for my imagination to prepare me for the sordidly microwaved meals in little boxes that were flung before the patrons of the dining car, and the floridly complexioned habitual drinkers slumped over in the bar car.

I made my way to the only vacant table and sat near the window, where I held a book up close to my face in hopes of discouraging anyone from misinterpreting my solitary status as an invitation for company and conversation. I could not concentrate on my reading, however, as the other diners were speaking loudly of their train-riding habits and their distrust of flying. This discouraged me further, as my own weakness in this area was what had caused me to throw in my lot with this company. If only I did not mind driving, or was not afraid of flying, I would not have been reduced to sitting in this airless room full of people, awaiting a tepidly microwaved cheeseburger in a small box made of thin cardboard.

Later that night, I wondered if I might not have been better served by eating nothing at all. The terrible taste of my meal had left pockets of residue in my mouth which I felt could not be banished simply by brushing my teeth. The small sink provided in my compartment was positioned directly above the toilet, a proximity which, although perhaps serving some purpose in terms of plumbing, was worrisome from the perspective of hygiene. I had read at one time that unusually small apartments in Tokyo also involved the nesting of various plumbing functions one atop the other, but I liked to imagine that in that context, felicitous design might have produced an overall effect of streamlined futurism, rather than creating in the user a sense of unease with regard to sanitation.

Plagued by the taste of cardboard and rewarmed beef, I

switched on the lamp above my head and took out my travel notebook and a volume on the Bauhaus movement. My mother had come into the city a few days before my departure to bid me farewell and loan me the book for my journey. "This might be useful," she had said. "I understand that James De Lourgnier is a scholar of Bauhaus architecture, and it is always nice to prepare oneself when meeting with learned people, I think."

"Yes, mother, I know," I had replied. It always irked me when she reminded me of social tenets that she had long before taught me, and that I always took pains to follow. "I am familiar with the rudiments of Bauhaus. But, it would be helpful to refresh my memory," I added, so as not to hurt her feelings.

"I know you are very knowledgeable about design, darling, but I thought this book might be helpful because it also introduces details about the history and the politics. I think that might impress your cousin James, don't you?"

"Is he really my cousin?" I asked, hoping to change the subject. Despite the knowledge that I was researching my grandfather's work, my mother persisted in thinking of me as purely enmeshed in aesthetic concerns, while I had, I felt, grown beyond this and had become more interested in precisely those issues which she felt it her duty to point out to me.

"Well, of course, he is not that closely related to you, but don't you think it's nicer to think of him as a cousin?"

"If he is my step-grandmother's great nephew, then I suppose that would make him my step second cousin. Yes, I see what you mean."

"It might be better when you meet him to simply refer to

him as a cousin," my mother ventured. "It seems nicer to me."

"But he is a scholar, Mother. Surely he is more interested in accuracy."

My mother sighed. She felt that my commitment to accuracy could put a damper on friendly conversations, whereas I felt that paving over important details for the sake of friendly communication could only introduce notes of falsity into one's interactions. We both knew that we would never be able to convince one another of our stances.

After perusing the Bauhaus book for some time, I switched off the light and lay back in the darkness, listening to the muffled clanking of the train. There was something else my mother had said during that conversation that had bothered me. She had already put on her coat and gloves, and was getting ready to leave my apartment, when she stopped and turned.

"Oh!" she said. "I forgot to tell you. I spoke with Ned yesterday and he said he saw your friend Roger the other day with that woman from Schiffley House."

"With Lucinda? But that can't be. She would have told me if she were planning a visit, and anyway, she's not at all partial to Roger."

"No, no, not Lucinda, the other one that you had dinner with. He described her as a black woman, very tall and quite good-looking."

"Antoinette?" I felt suddenly weak.

"Yes, I think that's it. He said they were walking into a restaurant. They didn't see him, and he rightly decided it was better not to approach them."

I was dumbfounded by this revelation. Though it had been clear that Roger had formed some kind of connection with Antoinette that night at the restaurant, I hadn't imagined that there would be more to it than that, or at least I had hoped not. More troubling than the fact of their meeting was the secretiveness of it. Roger had never shown any inclination to hide from me his trysts with women. What was he hiding now?

Since this conversation, I had tried to push the matter from my mind. I had met Roger for a cup of coffee the day before my departure and he had said nothing of Antoinette, though I had brought up her name several times in hopes of eliciting a confession. His face was a cipher; I could discern no indications that he was hiding a secret in his reactions to my words. Had Ned been mistaken?

Roger had shown little interest in any discussion of the Schiffley house and archivist, and had instead expressed an eagerness that I visit Graceland, the former home of Elvis Presley, when I passed through Memphis. Having little exposure to the music of Elvis Presley, and even less interest in what Roger cited as the "camp value" of Presley's former home, I was unenthusiastic at the prospect of such a detour. But Roger was quite insistent, and in the end managed to get me to promise to visit the house if only so that I might purchase a postcard and mail it to him. Turning these things over in my mind was making it difficult for me to fall asleep. I tried instead to focus my thoughts on my trip's goal, the table. This had the desired effect, and a feeling of deep peace washed over me.

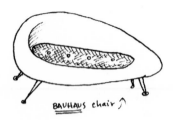

BAUHAUS chair ♪

14

I woke some time just before dawn, with a sudden jolt from the train resuming its course after a stop on the tracks. I was startled and unsure of my whereabouts for a moment. I lay quite still as I gathered my wits about me, and slowly reminded myself of the fact that I was on a train en route to Chicago, where I would spend the day, and that later I would journey to the South in search of the table.

As dawn broke, the daylight, filtered through the filthy green-tinted Plexiglas windows, revealed an unfamiliar landscape devoid of hill or tree. Fields of some crop stretched out for miles around. I had never considered what the Midwest might look like, but once glimpsed, I knew immediately that this was it. Perhaps if I had given more attention to American literature or painting, the bleak expanses of what I assumed were cornfields would not have been such a surprise to me. We were headed due west but I was seated facing east, and even the thick discolored panes of plastic could not lessen the surprising beauty of the pink-tipped dawn stretching out her fingers across the stalks of corn (or perhaps it was soy? I remembered reading somewhere that soy was an important crop in the Midwest).

The fascinating and novel view from my window, coupled with my continued indigestion from the meal the night before, helped to steel my resolve never to enter the dining car again. I reached over to my coat, which I had hung from the hook near the foot of the bed and fished out a small tin of saltines and cheddar slices I had packed before setting out, in case I needed a snack. This could be my breakfast, and on arriving in Chicago, where I would have to spend much of the day before the next train to Memphis, I could locate some local establishment with more wholesome food and take my lunch there. After eating a small portion of this snack and washing it down with the dregs of the coffee I had brought in a thermos the day before, I rose and performed my toilet as quickly as possible so as to avoid contact with the toilet and sink. Then I dressed in the small amount of space in which I could stand, and attempted to tidy up the bed linens and return the berth to its function as a seat, a task which proved beyond me. Giving up at last, I placed a pillow against the wall, and leaning against it, I settled down with the volume on Bauhaus and awaited my arrival in Chicago.

I must confess that Chicago was to me a revelation. Up until the moment I disembarked from the train, my knowledge of the city was based entirely on Upton Sinclair's book *The Jungle*, one of the few works of American literature that I had read. The work had been assigned in secondary school, and I had expected to be indifferent to it, but it left a profound impression on me. The cover did not promise much of interest, but I found myself riveted by the book. *The Jungle* had sent me on a lengthy series of experiments and research projects involving the production of meat, its smells and preparations and so on. As I learnt more about the field of animal husbandry and the conditions of slaughterhouses, I became overcome with revulsion for the consumption of meat, and I had adopted the habits of a vegetarian, eschewing meats, fish, and even dairy for a time. Eventually these eating restrictions became untenable in a boarding school caféteria, and my poor mother was beside herself as to how to provide me with proper nourishment. And so, after some months, I reverted to my carnivorous ways, though it must be said I never again regarded the visage of a large porterhouse steak with the same gusto.

This small glimpse into the history of Chicago did nothing to prepare me for the city that greeted me after I had climbed the station's grand staircase and stepped out into the sunshine. I imagined a day wandering among smokestacks and covering my nose with a handkerchief to avoid the fumes. Perhaps lunch at a hotdog stand and a brisk walk by the lakeside. Instead, I found myself instantly surrounded by immense edifices, some new and some old, clear evidence of a city that prospered and an architectural magnificence the likes of which I had not imagined. Enquiring of a passerby as to the direction toward the lake, which I knew to be east of the station, I set off down a wide street teeming with industrious people. Though the city in many ways reminded me of New York, it was altogether built on a larger scale. One had a sense of man's insignificance in the face of his own creations. I realized now that I thought of it that the Bauhaus book had made mention of Chicago as being home to many examples of that aesthetic. I wondered if any of the buildings I passed could be considered Bauhaus. I made my way down the street slowly, in awe, and quite nearly ran into other pedestrians on several occasions, and at one crosswalk slightly twisted my ankle at a high curb when I failed to look down.

Here and there I glimpsed a small eatery tucked between enormous doorways through which well-dressed men and women streamed in and out, full of tremendous and, no doubt, laudable purpose. I was becoming terribly hungry after forgoing breakfast, as I was accustomed to heartier fare for the first meal of the day, and though the saltines and cheese had staved off my hunger for a while, I now began to feel sharp pangs. Yet none of the dining establishments sufficiently piqued my interest to cause me to leave off my voyage of discovery as I marched eastward toward the lake. Eventually I came to a curious disjuncture in the magnificent landscape of towering gray stone and cement: a rusted metal structure, about two stories high, bisected my path. The structure was mounted on metal pillars, and upon closer observation, while still at the distance of some blocks, I noted that it was fitted with stair-cases, and that people were busily climbing up and down the stairs. Just then a train, similar in appearance to a subway car, pulled up atop the structure, and I realize that this must be the train track for the city's transit system. I was taken aback at the stark contrast between the awe-inspiring examples of architecture I had been admiring, and the rickety, unkempt appearance of the transit system. There was much about the city that I had yet to understand.

Crossing beneath this elevated transit structure, one felt transported to another city altogether. Suddenly one's eye was caught by a not insignificant degree of filth and disarray. Homeless persons crouched in corners, garbage cans over-flowed. The sun was blocked from this part of the street and I felt a chill run up my spine. An old man approached me with a newspaper in his hand. His teeth were decayed and his eyes rheumy, but his gait was firm and purposeful, and he managed to fairly block me from continuing on my way. I tried to push past him, but he thrust the paper in my face. I glanced at the cover. The price of one dollar was printed on the front.

"Very well," I said, taking a bill from my wallet. "Here you go, then." The man smiled widely with a ghastly grin that revealed his gums. He handed me the paper. I sucked in my breath and fancied I smelled some sort of processed meat sandwich wafting from his person. "Thank you, thank you," I muttered, as I continued briskly on my way. With just a few steps I had passed back into the stately domain that had disap-peared temporarily beneath the train tracks. I breathed a sigh and looked about. Up ahead the street appeared to dead-end into a large and impressive edifice. As I drew closer, I could see that it was clearly an art museum. Great banners advertising current exhibitions flapped in the air above the high doors. I would have to visit this museum, I thought, but my hunger was getting the better of me. Just then, I stopped at a marquis and carpet stretching out across the sidewalk. The sign in the window advertised a Russian tearoom.

I was nearly at the museum, and had imagined that I would take some lunch in the caféteria that was sure to be there, but the sudden appearance of the tearoom seemed almost a sign from providence. I could not believe my good fortune, but I worried that perhaps my preconceptions of what a Russian tearoom might be would not match up with the reality. I stepped closer to the building to see if a menu was posted on the outside. It was not. I pulled open the heavy glass door and went inside. The interior was accented with deep reds and pinks. The chairs were upholstered in burgundy plush and the wallpaper was covered with enormous red and pink roses. Wide, heavy gilt-framed mirrors hung on the side walls, creating in the somewhat narrow space the impression of endless vistas. Along the left wall were generously sized booths with banquettes upholstered in a similar fashion to the chairs. The décor was indeed promising, and I realized I must have become abstracted in its contemplation when an ivory-skinned young woman with reddish hair pulled back in a bun asked with some impatience, "Sir? Party of one, Sir?"

"Yes, yes, just one," I replied, abandoning my previous intention to inspect the menu first.

The young woman led me to a small table near the back, from which I had a view of the street, but I could also see into a side room, which appeared to be reserved for larger parties. I had been left with the menu, an enormous volume bound in dark red leather of a shade similar to the fabric covering the chairs. Between the covers of the menu was a vast world of delectable and unusual cuisines from areas spanning the entire former Soviet Union. I realized that despite the sharp pangs of hunger in my belly, it would take some time to peruse all the offerings. A heavy-set waitress approached my table several times, growing impatient by the third or fourth visit.

"Perhaps you'd like something to start with," she suggested, with, I thought, a hint of irritability in her tone. "An appetizer or something to drink?"

"Yes, yes," I responded. I was no more ready to order now than I had been before, but I feared at a busy establishment such as this there would be little patience for singletons such as myself lingering over the menu at the noontime hour. "Perhaps," I hesitated. "Perhaps I will take some of the herring... and these pumpkin dumplings to start?"

The waitress wrote the order rapidly. "Anything to drink, Sir?" She had a slight accent. I wondered if she were Russian, and wanted very much to ask, but her demeanor did not suggest openness to uninvited questions.

"I will take," I looked over the beverage list again, "I will take a pot of hot tea. Of Russian Caravan," I added, deciding to forego my usual Lapsang Souchong in favor of the selection that was most obviously in keeping with the milieu. After the waitress left, I wondered if, after all, this was the case. Was Russian Caravan really more Russian? Perhaps the title was misleading. I took out my notebook, entered the date, name of the restaurant and the city and state. Then I wrote, "How is Russian Caravan tea Russian?" I then returned to the riches of the menu. I noticed now that part of the heft of the menu was due to the fact that it also included selections for formal tea, dinner and a dizzying array of vodkas, including flavored vodkas and vodkas imported from a number of international distilleries in the former Soviet Bloc as well as in Scandinavia and Western Europe. As tempting as these selections were, I realized that midday between trains was not the time to sample a flight of vodkas, and I hastily flipped back to the luncheon menu.

Eventually I settled upon a sampler platter. The platter was quite expensive, but it included an impressive selection of small portions of dishes from throughout the rest of the menu, and would be, on the whole, far cheaper than ordering full dishes and eating only small portions, which was the alternative. Just as a wine taster manages never to grow intoxicated while practicing his craft, I had perfected the art of eating widely but sparingly, and only taking so much of a particular dish as might be needed to form an impression of its taste.

Though I did not engage in taste collection in any formal way at this stage in my life, such habits are difficult to shake, and I was still in the habit of taking notes on unusual dishes while eating. This habit had caused restaurant staff to mistake me for a critic on more than one occasion, a circumstance that worked distinctly in my favor. I was never overtly questioned as to my identity, but when the decision was taken somewhere in the kitchen that I might be a restaurant critic traveling incognito, I would suddenly find myself treated with a number of additional and complementary delicacies, some not even listed on the menu. I always take extra care to note down the qualities of these complementary treats, and I treasure the memory of each one.

On one occasion, for example, at an Asian fusion restaurant, I was treated to a small dish of the most delectable lime ginger shrimp with nasturtium blossoms, and on another, while dining at a small trattoria near my apartment, I was brought the most exquisite coconut sorbetto nested inside a coconut shell, accented with crushed candied pistachios. The sorbet was nowhere to be found on the menu. When I returned to the same establishment some months later in the company of my mother and a friend of hers visiting the city for some shopping, I had enquired about the dish and was told that the restaurant had never offered such a dessert. I felt flattered that the coconut sorbetto had apparently been produced for me alone.

On this occasion, I simply took notes in order to memorialize this part of my journey to the South. Due to the taciturn demeanor of the wait staff and the quickly growing crowd of well-heeled office workers rushing in for business lunches, I harbored no expectations of unexpected Russian delicacies materializing, *Brigadoon*-like, at my table. When I had finished writing down my first impressions, describing the location and recording my menu choices, I dug into my appetizers with enthusiasm and found them to be delicious and altogether unfamiliar. In the interlude between courses, as I sipped my tea, I picked up the newspaper I had so infelicitously purchased beneath the train tracks. Glancing over its pages, it became clear to me that the publication was dedicated to the cause of homelessness, a noble purpose. The ink, however, I found to be not fast, and my hands became smudged with the perusal of its pages. The writing, though full of fine feeling and worthy sentiments, left something to be desired in its style, and when my main course arrived, I was happy enough to fold the publication in half and set it to one side on the floor, where I must have probably left it when I later stood to leave the restaurant.

After a thoroughly satisfying sampler platter, I was replete, but I simply could not pass up the opportunity to taste a Russian Napoleon. The cream was delightfully flavored, but the pastry seemed rather dense. I wondered if the pastries were made in their kitchen, and if one could draw any conclusions from the Napoleon about Russian pastry-making, or if, more likely than not, the pastries were brought in from some outside patisserie, in which case it was unclear what conclusions should be drawn from this particular dish.

After settling my substantial bill, I visited the small, but surprisingly ornate bathroom. As I washed my hands in the sink, which was embedded in a counter top of pink-veined marble, accented with gold faucets that matched the golden fixtures on the toilet and the gold hand-towel rack, I glanced up at my reflection in the mirror, and was startled to see how disheveled I looked. Certainly, there had been no opportunity for a bath in the train, but I had wetted down my hair and combed and parted it neatly, and had even managed to shave while the train was moving. I now saw that these efforts had been imperfect, however, and that I had nicked my face in several spots where there were now small scabs forming. My hair looked greasy and tousled in spots. There were dark circles under my eyes from a fitful night of sleep. I wondered if my not discourteous, but abrupt treatment at the hands of the restaurant's staff might have been due to my unkempt appearance. Alas, there was nothing to do for it now, so I carefully washed the small cuts on my face and patted them dry with a paper hand towel. Over the piped-in Russian folk music, I could hear some men talking just outside the door, and I realized that a line was forming while I took the time to clean off my face and smooth down my hair with my fingers. I had checked my luggage at the station coatroom, and with it my comb and shaving kit, so temporary measures would have to do.

Outside the bathroom, I apologized to the gentlemen standing in line. They were prosperous portly men wearing tailored suits. I thought they must be bankers, or captains of industry. They appeared to be engrossed in conversation and had not minded after all my lengthy stay in the bathroom. Glancing at my wristwatch, I saw that it was nearly two-thirty, and I hurried out of the tearoom, through the heavy glass doors, and back into the sunlight, which felt strong after the dim lighting inside. Now I turned my steps quickly to the art museum, just half a block away.

JOHN the BAPTIST

15

That evening, as I sat in my new compartment bound for Memphis, I laid out across my pillow the postcards I had purchased at the gift shop in the museum. A Seurat for Lucinda, a Greek statue for Uncle Ned, a Chinese Buddha for my mother, who had recently developed an interest in Buddhism, and a Medieval Italian painting of Salomé requesting the head of John the Baptist for Roger. This last was part of a series that had most drawn my interest in the museum. I had made my way through the Greek and Roman antiquities because I knew Uncle Ned would ask for a report. I found the collection satisfying, but nowhere near as extensive as the one in Boston that I knew best. I had spent many rainy afternoons there in the company of my mother and Ned, who always took care to explain the mythology associated with his favorite pieces of ancient pottery and statuary.

From there, I made a quick tour of the galleries of Chinese

and Japanese art on behalf of my mother. The galleries them-
selves were done up in a splendid style. One felt a strange sense
of calm in a room designed like a small Buddhist temple, and
museumgoers sat on benches in quiet reverence until a large
group of school children burst through the doors and shat-
tered the quiet with their rowdy cries. At this juncture, I quick-
ly made my way to the upper galleries where I spent some time
with the Impressionist paintings, in this case, in order to tell
Lucinda what I had seen, as she was a great fan, especially of
pointillism. Pride of place was given in the exhibition to the
Seurat painting *A Sunday Afternoon on the Island of La Grande
Jatte*, of a man and woman promenading in the park. I regret
that I felt over-exposed to the work through reproductions on
calendars, T-shirts and the like, and, try as I might, I was un-
able to fully appreciate its probable fine qualities in a fresh way.

Growing fatigued with these galleries, which led to other
rooms dedicated to ever more modern eras, I had opened up
my floor map and located the Medieval and Renaissance pe-
riod. I retraced my steps and found that these rooms led off
from the original room in which the Seurat was showcased.
The presentation of that painting arrested one's attention so
thoroughly that I had not noticed the smaller, more dimly lit
corridors that led off to the sides.

Here, in the side rooms, among the crucifixes and Madon-
nas ornamented with dazzling haloes of gold-leaf and dramat-
ically embellished with the bright pigments of tempera paints,
I was most at home. The vibrant pallet of azures, crimsons and
ochres excited me, and the lighting, kept dim to preserve these

delicate masterpieces, soothed me after a morning of surprises and excitement. Renaissance painting had been my father's area of expertise, and as a child, I had spent many happy hours poring over his collection of art books on the floor of his study while he wrote. The museum's collection was small but full of rare and wonderful works that I had not previously seen. As always with this period of art, I marveled at the power of the artist's imagination. Surely Seurat had seen Parisians promenading in the park countless times, but had these medieval painters ever seen a man crucified? How did they know how to paint the wounds in Jesus' hands and feet; how did they imagine the quality of pain that might be etched in his countenance as he hung from the cross?

In these galleries I was particularly drawn to a series of six paintings by Giovanni di Paolo depicting the life and death of St. John the Baptist. In a magnificent scene in the fourth of these, Salomé requests of King Herod the head of John the Baptist. In the fifth, St. John's beheading is portrayed, and in the sixth, his head is presented to the court. I stood examining these last three for quite some time, in particular the scene of the beheading. Again I marveled at the creative genius of the painter. St. John's body was shown leaning out his prison window, his bloodied head held by a stooping guardsman. Streams of bright red blood pour like fountains from his headless neck, and his hands seem still to grasp the windowsill. Had the artist ever seen a beheading? Perhaps if he had not seen a human beheaded, he might have studied the slaughter of animals in order to perfect his portrayal of the martyring of St. John.

Realizing that the museum guard had begun to regard me with suspicion due to the length of time I was spending before this set of six paintings (what is known as a "hexaptych", I remembered my father telling me), I withdrew to a bench in the middle of the room, and wrote down my impressions in my notebook, even filling in some pages with crudely rendered sketches of the panels. By this time it was already four-thirty, and the museum would, I imagined, close at five o'clock. I shut my notebook and placed my pen in my pocket. After one more glance at each painting, I made my way down to the gift shop, where I purchased the postcards, and then to the restrooms, which I imagined would be more congenial than any I might find in the train station. Then, not wishing to find myself beneath the platform of the elevated train after dark, I returned the way I had come, stopping at a small café to purchase a sandwich for later on the train, as well as some bottled lemonade. Near the train station, I noticed a bookshop, which seemed promising at first, but proved to be rather unimpressive. Nonetheless, I was able to pick up a newspaper and volume of poetry by an American poet named Carl Sandburg, which would, according to the description on the back, illuminate the city of Chicago for me in unexpected ways.

In retrospect, as I now surveyed my postcards arrayed across the pillow, I was not sure why I had selected the Salomé painting for Roger. Neither was I convinced that he would appreciate it in the same way I did, nor was I entirely sure that he deserved it. In point of fact, now that I picked it up and examined it in my palm, I was quite sure that he did not. I resolved to keep the Salomé for myself, since I had already promised Roger a postcard from Graceland. Anyone who wanted the latter would have no use for the former, I reasoned. The hour was late, and although I would have liked to have written my postcards then, I knew from looking over my writing from the previous evening in the train that my penmanship could not withstand the jolting rhythm of the train. I carefully replaced the cards in the small paper bag from the museum gift shop and slipped the bag inside the Bauhaus book for safekeeping. Then I prepared for bed, turned down the sheets, and lay down with the volume of poetry by Carl Sandburg. I found the poetry to have a soporific effect, or perhaps it was just the fatigue of the day's adventures catching up with me. Finding myself drifting off to sleep, I closed the book, put it on the small rack near the berth and switched off the light.

standard BREAKFAST
(Oxford, MS)

16

That night, I again slept fitfully, partly out of anxiety that I would not wake up in time for the early morning arrival at the station, and partly out of a lingering fear of an intrusion into my compartment, though I was not sure what or whom I expected. On both counts it appeared I had nothing to fear, for no one intruded on my slumbers during the night, and the sleeper attendant rang the bell on my compartment a full half an hour before our arrival in Memphis, waiting until I had slid open the door and presented myself as fully awake before he went on his way.

After disembarking at the station, I hastened to the information kiosk to learn more about hiring a car to take me to Oxford. Unfortunately, it was not yet seven in the morning, and the kiosk was not scheduled to open until eight. Slightly anxious, I proceeded out to the front of the station in hopes of finding a taxi. There were in fact a few taxis lined up in front, perhaps anticipating the arrival of this particular train. I had no success in convincing the first two to take me the eighty or so miles to Oxford, but the third driver agreed, on the condition that I pay a hefty surcharge. The car was stuffy and smelled strongly of tobacco mingled with stale coffee. My driver was a taciturn man, which suited my state of exhaustion. It was unfortunate that he had a taste for call-in radio programs, but thankfully the Southern accents of the callers were thick enough that I could not make out the topic under discussion without much effort. As the car pulled out of the city and drove through farmlands, I nodded off to sleep. When I awoke, it was mid-morning and we had arrived in Oxford.

The driver dropped me off at a small pension in the center of town, where I had reserved a room. I checked into the room, bathed and dressed, and then sat down to read more of the volume on Bauhaus and take some notes. I felt it was important to be prepared for my meeting with James. At one in the afternoon, I took a stroll about town and was lucky to happen upon a small café where tea and some light pastries were available. Afterwards, I sought out a post office, where I could mail all my cards save the one of Salomé, and then I returned to my room for an afternoon nap. When I awoke, it was close to five, and, as had been arranged, I telephoned James and informed him of my arrival in town. He said that he would come and fetch me at six.

Jim, as he asked me to call him when we met, was of medium height and unprepossessing appearance. I had imagined something different from a scholar of Bauhaus, though I am not sure why. Perhaps a Germanic look, or some physical manifestation of a preoccupation with the sleek, streamlined style of the movement he studied. Jim had an ordinary appearance, though the frames of his glasses did seem fashionable and his shoes may have been of a more expensive type than those of the average scholar.

Jim expressed interest in the fact that I had chosen to make a train journey to visit him. "How long does that take?" he asked. "Two days?"

I nodded.

When he asked why I had not simply flown to see them, I was forced to explain that I suffered from a fear of flying, a topic I did not particularly wish to discuss. He made the unoriginal observation that my fear of flying was ironic. This supposed irony was rarely lost on those who learned of my phobia: the grandson of the inventor of the jet engine has only once sat on an airplane! The notion always amused people, as though there were some inherent contradiction; as if my distrust of being carried aloft in a giant metal airship could have anything to do with my genealogical link to one of our nation's greatest inventors. Of course I was ashamed when I wondered at times what my grandfather would have thought of my weakness. But to me the fear was rooted in my great reverence for his invention. The power of the jet engine was beyond comprehension. I would no more avail myself of its force for a routine journey than I would attempt to climb on the back of an eagle to soar into the sky.

After a fifteen-minute drive, Jim pulled up in front of a

small pale green bungalow. Just inside the front door, he took off his shoes and placed them on a rack, after which I followed suit. I was glad I had selected a newer pair of socks that did not require any darning. Hearing the sounds of our arrival, Jim's wife, Cherise, came out to greet us.

As Cherise held out her hand to me, I was momentarily taken aback at her great beauty, which stood in stark contrast to Jim's indifferent demeanor. I was also surprised by how informally she was dressed. She wore an old athletic shirt and sweatpants with slippers. She was tall, thin and angular and appeared to be Asian. A few moments later, when she brought some hors d'oeuvres into the room—a ripe Brie, wheat thins and a spread made of preserved figs—I was startled yet again by her attire. In my mind's eye, I had re-clothed her in a tasteful black sheath and perhaps backless sandals. She must have seen the startled look on my face, for she said, mistaking the source of my surprise, "Oh, I'm sorry to surprise you! When I wear these," she said, pointing to her slippers, "I walk very quietly and have a tendency to sneak up on people." She giggled.

Seated on a low boxy sofa covered in gray canvas and accented by a few black and white throw pillows, I gazed about the living room, the walls of which were almost completely covered in many rows of books. The coffee table was sleek and modern with a glass top and a metal frame. I had hoped to catch a glimpse of the fruit table in the living room, but clearly it would have looked out of place in this setting. Perhaps they kept it in a study or bedroom.

On the coffee table, I was pleased to see in a pile of works concerning architecture and design the same volume on the history of Bauhaus that my mother had lent me. My mother was, after all, always correct in the matter of social graces. After some small talk about my journey, during which Jim darted in and out as he attended to the dinner preparations, it was announced that the meal was ready, and we made our way into the dining room.

The perfectly white walls of the dining room were covered with examples of some sort of Oriental calligraphy, an area about which I must confess I have no knowledge whatsoever.

Jim served the meal with some pride; he was the cook in the family, it seemed. It was simple fare, consisting of a delicately roasted chicken, pilaf and salad. After I had commended him on his cooking, I complimented Cherise on the beauty and artistry of the calligraphy lining the walls.

"Oh, the calligraphy?" Cherise smiled indulgently and passed me a pitcher of ice water. "That's all Jim's. I don't have an artistic bone in my body."

"Oh, I'm sorry! I guess I assumed it was your work."

"Because I'm Asian?"

"Yes, I imagine so."

"I'm actually Korean—that's Japanese. Jim spent a few years studying Japanese calligraphy in Tokyo long before we met."

"I just love the simple design element. That writing—a functional activity—could produce a wonderfully pure design aesthetic." Jim added, "It's what led me eventually to Bauhaus."

I glanced from Jim to Cherise.

"People always think it's my work," laughed Cherise. "I can't say I mind getting all the credit. They're beautiful, aren't they?"

I nodded. "Might I ask then, what sort of work you do? Are you also a scholar?"

"Cherise is a leading Faulkner scholar," said Jim proudly, patting her on the shoulder.

"Faulkner...oh! And I believe he was a resident of Oxford, was he not?" I was thankful that before coming to their house I had leafed through a local guidebook I had found on the shelf in the room where I was staying.

"Oh, yes," said Cherise. "Working at Ole Miss is nirvana for Faulkner scholars. The archive is amazing!"

"I'm embarrassed to say I've only read one Faulkner story, in high school," I said. "It was a macabre tale concerning a woman who never married, and I think it was later discovered that her fiancé was lying dead in an upstairs room?"

"That's 'A Rose for Emily.' Everyone reads that in high school," laughed Cherise.

I felt ashamed at my shallow knowledge of Faulkner's work, and yet again regretted my lack of interest in American literature. A great author, of whose oeuvre I had only read one short story typically studied by high school students! I made a mental note to invest some time in reading the major novels of William Faulkner.

"Cherise heads her own research institute here, so there was no question of whether we should move here, but it's been hard, adjusting to living in the Deep South," remarked Jim. "We were at the University of Minnesota before," he added.

The conversation turned for a time to Cherise's research, until she abruptly changed the topic.

"But Jim, aren't you going to ask your cousin about his letter?"

"Oh yes, I'm so sorry! We don't get many visitors here, so we were just enjoying the conversation! But—wait, are we cousins? I guess so..."

"Oh wait, wait! Let me get a pen!" Cherise rushed out of the room and then returned with a notebook and a pen. "Let's see. She was your aunt? Daniel's grandmother? Is that right?"

I was slightly confused. I began to explain the relationship haltingly. Jim broke in. "Cherise has a graduate student in anthropology—"

"—he's studying southern patterns of kinship through Faulkner's novels. We've been doing a lot of genealogy mapping at the Institute. I'm learning how to do it. It's kind of fun."

She started writing, but suddenly dropped her pen, and slapping her hand on her forehead, she said, "Look at me, I brought the conversation right back round to Faulkner again! You were supposed to be telling us your questions. Jim, why didn't you stop me?"

Jim looked at her lovingly and brushed a strand of hair away from her eyes. "Cherise is so passionate about her work," he said, lost in the contemplation of his wife's beauty for a moment.

"But, yes, you mentioned, in your email, something about

Aunt Jane's bequests? She was my great aunt by the way," he said to Cherise.

Now that the moment had finally come to ask about the fruit table, I felt frozen with fear. The idea that the table might be in the same house where I sat was overwhelming. For a moment there was silence. I looked down at my plate. Only a few grains of rice and a chicken bone remained. Though simple, the meal had been surprisingly refreshing, especially after my long journey. I pushed the remaining grains of rice onto my fork with my knife. I needed courage. My mission seemed more difficult to explain than I had anticipated, and I began to wish I had simply asked about the table in my message. I took a large sip of wine and struggled to begin the story.

For a while it did not seem as though Jim and Cherise could follow what I was saying. They both sat, looking quizzically at me, and quietly sipping their wine. At last it seemed as though Jim had understood, and he broke in.

"Oh that awful table! I had almost forgotten about that—" he stopped short of finishing the sentence when he saw me gazing at him in horror.

"I'm so sorry—it's a design thing—the Victorian era, so over the top. It just doesn't do it for me. But," he cleared his throat and took a sip of wine, "but I can see that you feel differently about it."

"It was a beautiful piece of craftsmanship," I said, after a pause. I worried that my face was betraying my emotions too much. I felt myself blushing.

"To be sure, to be sure. Honestly, I never saw it in person,"

Jim replied. "I was sent a photograph. I can see it would have some camp value, but it really wouldn't fit in with my taste," he said, gesturing with his hand generally to indicate the evidence of his taste that lay around us in the room. "I had it shipped to an antique dealer in New York. Got a pretty nice payment for it as well."

I was stunned. At that moment I felt hatred for Jim and Cherise and their smiling faces, but I knew, rationally, that this was not justified. They had not known the table, nor, it seemed, had Jim known Grand Jane at all. There was no history, no sentiment attached to the table for him. Moreover, the table simply did not fit in with his aesthetic sensibilities, much as it had been a misfit amongst my grandfather's furnishings. I could not blame my grandmother for her bequest to Jim. Perhaps she had never meant for him to keep the table, and had intended to benefit him financially all along; and I had never spoken a word about the table to her that I recalled. All the same, I found myself speechless. I wanted to be alone so that I could experience my anguish privately.

After a long and uncomfortable silence, I wiped my mouth with my napkin and placed it on the table. "I'm afraid it's getting late," I said. "You have been most hospitable, and I am very grateful for the meal. It was lovely. Perhaps," I added, "if it's not too much trouble, you could call a taxi cab for me. I don't want to trouble you any further."

I rose from my seat, stepped to one side and pushed the chair in at the table. Jim and Cherise looked surprised and slightly uncomfortable, but it couldn't be helped.

"No, no, it's no trouble!" Jim hurriedly stood up. "I can drive you back. But won't you stay for dessert and coffee? I made a pecan torte."

As tempting as this offer sounded, I knew I could not stay a moment longer.

"Thank you very much, it sounds delicious." I said, "but I really must be going now." I reached out my hand to Cherise. "Thank you so much for your hospitality. I had a lovely time." Then I turned and walked swiftly to the front hall where my coat was hanging and I had left my shoes. I heard my hosts talking in hushed voices in the other room. As I was tying my laces, Jim came out into the hall and picked up his keys.

"Shall we go, then?" he asked with a smile.

"Campy" Chair
(GRACELAND)

17

Back in my room, I paced for some time, unsure of what to do next. Jim had assured me he would look for the name of the antiques dealer through whom he had sold the table, but my hopes for this were not high. I did not know what upset me more: that I had made this difficult trip only to find the table gone, perhaps forever; or that Jim, clearly a man of discernment and good taste, had shown such a dismissive attitude toward the bequest. It had 'camp value.' How could such an exquisite piece of craftsmanship be summed up with the same dubious valuation as Roger had accorded Graceland? This thought reminded me that I had reluctantly promised Roger I would visit the former estate of Elvis Presley on my way home from Oxford. I was hardly in the mood to see a grand monument to the 'camp' aesthetic so soon after my experiences of that evening. Moreover, given Roger's all but certain deceit toward me with regard to his interactions with Antoinette, I was less than convinced that I should make any detours on his account at all.

That night I again slept poorly, waking frequently and turning my conversation with Jim over and over in my mind. Whenever I thought of his reference to the 'camp value' of the table, my mind would turn to Roger and, to what I began to feel was a betrayal of our friendship. Rising early the next morning, I bathed and then went to the sitting room and asked my hostess at the pension if she could arrange for a car to take me to Memphis. In the sitting room, I ate a small breakfast of toast and a boiled egg with tea and white grapefruit juice. Returning to my room, I packed my suitcase. The clasp on the suitcase, a piece from my father's old luggage set which was embossed with his monogram in gold on the sides, was coming loose again. I had hoped it would hold for the rest of the journey.

An hour later, a car arrived for me. I hurriedly settled my bill and loaded my suitcase into the trunk. All the way to Memphis, I hardly noticed the scenery nor the driver, a middle-aged woman, who gave up trying to start a conversation after a couple of attempts. I had no interest in discussing the weather or the successes of local sports teams. When we reached the train station, I paid the fare, removed my suitcase, and walked into the waiting room. It was only then, glancing at the television screens listing arrival and departure times, that I realized I had forgotten that my train was not due to depart until ten o'clock at night. In my haste to leave Oxford, I had neglected this important detail, and now I was left with fully ten hours on my hands and a decidedly nervous frame of mind that would have make it difficult for me to simply sit on a bench and read.

After walking around the waiting room a few times and glancing at the publications at the newsstand and at the refreshments available at the small snack counter, I stopped before a poster for Graceland. I felt angry with Roger just looking at this piece of poorly designed publicity and the photographs of the ridiculously gaudy interior of the house. Ah, but it was camp! Very well then, I thought. I will go and experience this 'camp value' in which everyone finds so much amusement. I would view the house and purchase the postcard I had promised Roger, and then I would return and dine somewhere close to the station. It was a fateful decision, and not one taken in a sound frame of mind. When I look back at what transpired since then, it is clear to me that had I not gone to view the Graceland mansion in Memphis, things might have gone better for me in the long run.

And so I went. I felt almost tearful on the taxi ride back to the station. After the ghastly excesses of rooms on public display at Graceland ("opulence," as it was described in a brochure) I was unable to contemplate eating anything when I returned to the station. I sat instead for some time on a bench, experiencing waves of nausea that overtook me with each recollection of the tour. At times I would pace. I purchased a newspaper, but did not read it. Eventually I bought a chocolate bar, a sandwich wrapped in cellophane and a bottle of orange juice for later, should I regain my appetite on the train ride to Chicago.

When the train finally arrived, I sat in my compartment and did not venture forth. I assumed the dining car would be closed. I would have been happy to have a drink, and was almost tempted to go to the bar car, but it was quite late at night, and I had begun to feel hungry. I attempted to eat what I could of the sandwich—egg salad—for nourishment. As I picked at the crumbs on the plastic wrapping, I gazed out into the darkness through the scratched window, and imagined the receding southern landscape.

I was exhausted, but knew it was fruitless to attempt sleep. I opened up my notebook to record my thoughts. I had intended to write about Graceland, about my disgust at the tawdry furnishings that were meant to convey a sense of luxury, but instead provided evidence of a gaping, empty soul. In a calmer frame of mind, I might have even made a list of the rooms and described their contents and their effect on me. I would have critiqued the tour, the labeling of the displays and the items available in the gift shop. But try as I might, I simply could not bring myself to describe even a single chandelier. Instead, my heart was filled with increasing rage at Roger, who, knowing me as well as he did, had blithely sent me on this errand for a postcard. A postcard!

I took out the postcard in question, which I had slipped between the pages of the Bauhaus book. The postcard showed a sitting room furnished with two asymmetrical chaises longues upholstered in magenta, where one was to rest one's back, and white, across the long seating area. The chaises longues were joined to form a sort of curvy "L" shape. Next to the chaises longues was a magenta armchair, and these three items were all grouped around a hideous coffee table with a glass top and large base made of three flat white curlicues. All these furnishings were placed on an indigo carpet with a wide leopard print margin. The walls were alternately painted apricot and lavender. I had admittedly chosen a card that I thought would make a rather pointed statement to Roger. Perhaps, upon seeing the grotesque interior design pictured on the card, he would realize that he had erred in sending me to Graceland. I did not necessarily hope for an apology, but perhaps a modicum of regret.

I turned the card over and thought of what to write. I would keep it short, due to the motion of the train. I wrote:

> Dear Roger,
> Here is the postcard of Graceland, as promised. It is indeed replete with 'camp value,' as you had indicated. It is a value that is unfortunately lost on this correspondent. The weather has been sunny, and quite warm in comparison to New England at this time of year.
> Sincerely yours,
> Daniel

As I wrote, the train did lurch several times, forcing me to produce an example of penmanship that was not up to my usual standards. In some areas there were smudges where my hand had slipped.

FLIGHT OF VODKA
(SAMPLE #)

18

Arriving in Chicago a bit after nine in the morning, I went first to the station bathroom to shave, so as not to repeat my previous mistake of shaving in a moving train. I took my suitcase with me as it contained my shaving kit. After relieving myself in a poorly maintained stall, I set up my shaving materials at a sink and set to work. Though I was no longer hampered by the constraints I had faced in the compartment, I had not anticipated my anxiety with regard to shaving in a public place. At that hour, the tail end of the commuter crowd was streaming through the station, and the toilets were in high demand, with large numbers of men in dark suits and lightweight fall coats entering and exiting the facility. I found myself turning my head every time the door opened, and then looking away quickly for fear that someone might think I was trying to catch their eye. This inevitably resulted in some nicks on my chin and my upper lip. I washed my shaving implements with care and set them about the sink, and then returned to one of the toilet stalls to fetch a few sheets of toilet paper with which to stanch the small traces of blood on my face.

I now had the distinct impression of drawing stares from the men entering the room. I turned and looked at myself in the mirror to see if there was something untoward about my appearance. I looked slightly disheveled since I had had no bath, but there seemed to be nothing especially noticeable to attract attention. I pressed a long sheet of toilet paper against my cuts, then hurriedly folded up the paper, placed it in the trash and packed up my shaving kit. I repacked the kit into my suitcase and shut the clasp. As I lifted the suitcase by the handles, half the clasp snapped off. It had finally broken. I was convinced that the Bauhaus book was the culprit. It was a large, heavy book, and the case was certainly not intended for the transport of such articles. I knelt down and put my arms around the suitcase to hug it shut. Then I stood up and carried it in this manner, close to my chest, out of the bathroom. A gentleman entering the bathroom was kind enough to hold the door for me.

At the luggage check, I asked the attendant if he had anything with which I might keep the suitcase firmly shut. There was no tape to be found behind the counter, but he was finally able to locate a stout length of twine, which we wound around the case several times and knotted. I checked the case and then asked for directions to the nearest post office, after which I set off on my walk through the city.

The post office was nearby and I was able to mail my postcard to Roger without much of a detour. It was now a little past ten, and still too early to visit the Russian tearoom, so I thought I would walk to the lake. On this occasion, only a few days later than my previous visit, the fall weather seemed to be giving way to a wintry chill. It was late October and the sun was nowhere to be seen. A stiff breeze emanated from the direction of the lake, and by the time I had reached the art museum, I decided to return to its collections rather than subject myself to a chilly stroll by the waterside.

Looking through the visitor's guide, I found that there was a section of the museum devoted to furniture, so I went first to those galleries. The furniture of course made me feel despondent about my ill-fated trip to find the table, so I hurried through, only lingering to examine a few of the finer pieces. I then proceeded to an exhibit of miniature replica rooms in the basement of the museum. Though these tiny rooms also contained furnishings, some even reminiscent of the style and era of the fruit table, I all the same found the rooms, reproductions of the interior design of various periods by a Mrs. James Ward Thorne, utterly delightful. I was entranced, for example, by *New York Parlor, 1850-70*, a room furnished in a style reminiscent of sections of Schiffley House, or certain stately homes now open to the public in Newport.

I was delighted by this dreamy little world of replicas, and became lost in the delicacy and detail of each tiny tableau. I wished my mother were there to see them, as I knew she would have been quite pleased by the work of Mrs. James Ward Thorne. At long last, feeling visually sated, but rather hungry, I glanced at my wristwatch and saw to my surprise that it was already half-past twelve. The tearoom would be open. I hurried up to the lobby and out of the museum.

When I cast my mind back to the events of my trip, looking for mistakes I might have made, I regret that the drinks I ordered at the tearoom for lunch that day were in point of fact excessive for the occasion, though they were extremely enjoyable at the time. I have long felt that taking drink at midday does not suit me, but I was unable to resist the temptation of the tearoom's flights of vodka this time. I was fatigued and troubled by my trip to Oxford, and had not eaten much in the past day and a half. It was, as my mother would say "the thin end of the wedge." There were many such flights to choose from. I selected the flavored combination of coriander, black currant tea and lime. Unfortunately, I began the flight before my food had come out, and was already slightly dizzy by the time I began to eat. My face felt warm, and I drank a glass of ice water to cool myself down. I began to notice, and feel peeved by, the volume of the Russian music being piped in along the wall to the right of my chair. I searched for the speaker, hoping to muffle the sound with a napkin, or my knee, but was unable to find the source of these irritating strains of the polka. I desisted from this activity when I noticed a waiter eyeing me suspiciously, but my irritation continued to mount. I didn't care for the strudel I ordered for dessert, and the tea felt tepid.

After settling the check, I made my way to the restroom, where I was horrified to discover that the button on my woolen trousers was missing. This was not, I hasten to add, a sign of my overeating, but rather likely due to the vintage of the trousers, which had been passed on to me by Uncle Ned. Ned had decided a few years before to hand down to me all his tailored clothing from his younger days that had long since grown too tight for his increasingly portly frame.

I wondered where the button had gone. It would be difficult to replace with the right type of button, as the trousers were at least fifty years old. After washing my hands, I returned to the dining room and asked a waiter if I might search under the table for a missing button. There was already a couple seated at my former table. The waiter looked displeased. He spoke to the couple in a hushed voice. The woman seated in my former chair stood up and looked over at me. She eyed me up and down with a look of disdain on her face, and picking up a large shiny black purse, she stepped aside from the table and waited for me to search. I approached the table and pulled out the chair. Kneeling down I looked around on the carpet, which was a dark red, patterned with small golden flowers. I tried to remember the color of the button. The trousers were brown, so the button must have been brown as well. I smoothed my hand along the area of the carpet beneath the chair. I could feel the woman's eyes boring into the back of my head. There seemed to be nothing there. I could have lost it anywhere: at the museum, the post office, or even the train station. I recalled that it had still been in place, though loose, at the train station when I had used the toilet there. I stood up, bowed to the woman whom I had displaced, and stepped away from the table, making room for her to return to her seat. She studiously looked away from me as she returned to her seat. The waiter also avoided meeting my gaze as I left.

I felt ashamed at the state of my trousers and wondered if I should buy a belt. Instead of crossing the street to the museum, I wandered up the main boulevard looking for a shop that might sell a belt. As I walked, I tried always to keep my arms at my sides to prevent my trousers from sliding down. Eventually, I found a small shop that specialized in men's neckties. They also had a limited inventory of belts. The prices for all of these items seemed extraordinarily high. On careful consideration, I wasn't sure if after all I had ever purchased a belt. Most of my clothing came from Ned, and the rest had been supplied by my mother, whenever she had perceived some shortcoming in my wardrobe. I wondered if a new belt was a justifiable expense. I tried on a simple, relatively well-made belt of brown cowhide. I felt that the saleslady noticed the absence of a button on my trousers, and in her silent gaze, I read deep disapproval. Once the belt was on, I felt a strong sense of relief, and decided to make the purchase right away however costly it might be.

I felt hot about the temples from the flight of vodka, but the heat seemed pleasant in a way as I walked back down the boulevard in the chilly late autumn breeze. There was a small café along the way that served wine and I wondered if perhaps a little more to drink might keep me warm. There were six hours left until my train departed. I entered the café and ordered a glass of wine at the counter, as well as a large oatmeal raisin cookie, so as not to appear to be there simply for the drink. The cookie would do for a snack later in the evening. I sat at a small round table near the window and watched the pedestrians walking briskly to and fro. The wine was not bad, and it revived me somewhat.

Feeling it was time to return to my thoughts on the table, I took out my notebook. When I opened it, my ticket to Graceland fell out and my sense of well-being immediately shattered. I thought not just of Roger's betrayal of my aesthetic sensibilities—what I had always felt to be in many ways our shared aesthetic—but also his betrayal of my trust. It was all but certain that he must be engaged in some sort of dalliance with Antoinette. How could it not be so? And yet they were so poorly matched. And why had he kept this a secret from me? My notes became scrawled and incoherent, and my mood was degenerating. I quickly downed the rest of my wine and hurried back out into the late afternoon, turning my steps toward the museum.

Back inside, I had meant to return to the miniature rooms, which I had found so soothing in the morning, but instead I found myself striding toward the medieval galleries. After a bit of searching, I again found the series of six paintings on the life of St. John the Baptist that I had admired on my previous stop in Chicago. The museum would close in an hour. I decided to spend ten minutes examining each panel, or maybe nine minutes, to allow time to walk down the stairs to the lobby before closing. Admittedly this was not the best way to calm myself down either. The subject matter was disturbing, and despite the beauty of the colors and the artistry, the depiction of violence was graphic. The guard for these galleries stayed close by, as if worried I might reach out and grab one of the panels. At one point she even asked me to step back a bit from the paintings. At ten to five, the closing bell sounded. I put on my overcoat, which was draped over my arm, and headed out of the museum and back toward the train station.

19

Arriving at the station, I found I still had four hours left until my train departed. I went outside and walked aimlessly around, but by then it had grown dark and a light drizzle made strolling unpleasant. Thankfully I noticed a small Irish pub, brightly lit and inviting, and went in and sat down at the end of the bar. The room was crowded with those same commuters from morning, now loosening their ties and sharing a drink before boarding their evening trains to points outside the city. I ordered a very nice glass of whiskey with a small dish of pretzels and sat admiring the gleaming wood of the bar and the paneling that adorned the walls of the pub. On my walk back from the museum, I had purchased two magazines, new issues of *The New Yorker* and *National Geographic*, hoping to pass the hours of my wait with these congenial publications. I thought they would help me soothe my nerves and push to one side the considerations of the deceit of Roger and the negligence of

Jim. Unfortunately, this hope proved illusory.

Seated at the bar, I pulled the *The New Yorker* from the pocket of my overcoat, and began to flip through the pages. In that single issue of the magazine, I counted no less than ten instances in which the word 'camp,' or 'campy,' was used! The term was used twice in the listings of happenings about town with reference to an art exhibition, and once regarding a cabaret performance. It was then used in two cartoons. Following this, there was some respite in an article on contemporary politics, but this was only the lull before the storm: an eight page article discussed a new female performing artist who was described as a 'neo-burlesque sensation,' and whose person and work were called 'camp' or 'campy' six times. Worse yet, the cartoon on the very next page pictured a particularly corpulent Elvis Presley stretched out on a chaise longue that looked remarkably similar to the one pictured on the postcard I had sent to Roger.

I closed the magazine in disgust and pulled the *National Geographic* from my other pocket. Here there was little chance of encountering references to the aesthetic of camp. For a time, I was pleased with my choice. I read an interesting article on the deforestation of the Amazon and another regarding religious shrines in Bhutan, during which time I also ordered a second glass of whiskey and asked for another dish of pretzels. My peace was not to last, however. The third article in the magazine concerned agriculture and famine in the Horn of Africa and quoted liberally from Dr. Minerva Green, née Schiffley, and her husband. On one page there was even a large glossy photo of Professor Green, her lovely face lined with concern, as she crouched in a field. In one hand, she held up a handful of very dry soil, in the other, two or three very small tubers. There was nothing for it but to stop reading. I paid for my drink and left *The New Yorker* on the bar, but took the *National Geographic*, knowing my mother would wish to see the article that quoted Minerva Green.

Walking out into the street, I felt slightly dizzy. I had only a few blocks to walk to the station, and then I would uncheck my suitcase and wait for the train. This I managed to accomplish without incident. Returning from the luggage check with my suitcase hugged to my chest, I sat down at the end of a long wooden bench and prepared for my wait. I neglected my usual practice of keeping reading or writing material open on my lap, however, something that helps one avoid untoward conversations in public places. Because of this oversight, I was soon enough approached by an unusually tall thin man of very pale complexion, who wore a cheaply made light grey suit.

"Mind if I sit here?" he asked, as he perched gingerly on the bench right next to me in preference to the vast, empty expanse of bench available to him.

I smiled faintly and looked away. He remarked then on the weather, and the changing of the seasons; unoriginal observations, in response to which I politely nodded and avoided eye contact. Then he withdrew a large heavy book from a voluminous shoulder bag made of homespun sackcloth, and asked if I would like to take a look. I did not wish to take a look, but he held it out across my lap, and I took it, mostly in the hopes that he would withdraw his long bony hand from my general vicinity.

"It contains all the answers to the world's problems," he said with a peaceful smile. "In fact, all the answers to the universe's problems," he added with emphasis.

I opened the book and was faintly repelled by the strange layout of the pages, a cacophony of words and images, italics and bold-faced print, all jumbled together with cartoonish illustrations of what appeared to be deities, mortals and many large white horses.

"Thank you," I said, shutting the cover and handing it back to him. I noticed as he took the book that his hair seemed slightly off-kilter, and realized that he must be wearing a wig. The man took my prolonged gaze as encouragement and offered to sell me the book for the price of ten dollars.

"No, thank you," I responded. "I have no room in my luggage for anything that large."

Not easily discouraged, he removed from his bag a set of small pamphlets whose cover designs were remarkably austere in comparison to the book.

"No problem," he said, "why don't you take some of these?"

"I'm sorry, but I really don't wish to buy anything at the moment," I replied.

"Free of charge," he said, with a wide smile. "Hari om," he added.

"Well, thank you," I said stiffly, taking the pamphlets and stuffing them into my pocket. I turned my head and looked away to signal that our conversation had come to an end. I was surprised to see at that very moment a man letting go of a baby carriage at the top of the large sweeping staircase that marked the entrance of the station. The baby carriage went bouncing horribly down the steps as everyone stood by watching it, seemingly unconcerned. Then the man took out a large gun and proceeded to fire it at a number of passersby, all of whom fell to the ground. Horrified, I stood up, wondering if there was something I should do.

"They're filming a commercial," said the man, still sitting next to me on the bench. "It's a re-enactment from a scene of a famous film that was shot here."

"Oh. I see." I sat down, my heart still pounding from watching a baby plunge to its death. The carriage was lying on its side at the bottom of the staircase, a baby doll lying nearby, and I now noticed the film crew and a profusion of film lights gathered to one side at the foot of the stairway. The victims of the shooting were all standing up now, dusting off their clothes.

"It's all maya," the man explained with a knowing smile. "The illusion of the material world."

"I see," I said, fixing my gaze on my hands clasped in my lap, willing the man to go away.

"Well, I must be going," he said, after a long silence. "It's been great talking to you. I'm Ram Lal, by the way." He held the palms of his hands together. "Namaste."

I looked up to nod a farewell, but he was already walking away, looking for a new target.

For half an hour or more, I watched the filming of the

commercial. Over and over the man would let go of the carriage and begin shooting as it bounced down the long flight of stairs. I wondered what product one could possibly advertise in such a manner. Certainly nothing related to children or babies. Eventually the spectacle was repeated so many times that it became boring. I absentmindedly fished the oatmeal raisin cookie from my pocket. I was beginning to have a headache from all the alcohol I had consumed and the beads of perspiration that had formed on my face had grown cold. I mopped my brow with a handkerchief, and pulled part of the plastic wrapping off the cookie. It was a very large cookie and I didn't think I would be able to eat the entire thing in one sitting. Picking at it slowly, I again turned to watch the falling baby carriage. My attention was so fixed on the commercial that I did not notice for a moment that the man seated on the bench behind me was trying to get my attention.

He was a young man of unkempt appearance who could have greatly benefited from the use of a razor and comb. He wore in one ear multiple tiny golden earrings and was dressed in the kind of leather jacket one might see on an aviator of a certain era. I could not right away make out what he was saying, but imagined it concerned the baby carriage.

"It's for a commercial," I said briskly. "It's not a real baby carriage."

The young man laughed and repeated what he had been saying. It suddenly occurred to me that he was trying to sell me drugs.

"What makes you think I would want to buy anything like

that from you?" I asked, trying to muster a modicum of indignation, but wondering, on the other hand, what it was that he might have.

"Doesn't hurt to ask, right?" he said with a smile that made him look altogether less trustworthy than he had before, when I had imagined he might be a student on a cross-country trip.

"At any rate, I don't suppose you'd have anything I wanted," I added.

The young man listed his inventory, which was surprisingly large. I had hardly ever acquired powder from anyone I hadn't known, and certainly not from a seller who had not been recommended by a friend or acquaintance. I hesitated.

The young man waited patiently, anticipating that he might make a sale. I had lived through nearly two days of constant anxiety and frustration, and the alcoholic beverages I had consumed on this day had done little to focus my nerves. Thus, I succumbed to temptation and ordered a relatively small quantity of powder, just enough to tide me over for the next few days. Having made my purchase, I cast one last glance at the filming of the commercial. The crew was packing up. I picked up my suitcase and hugging it to my chest to keep it from coming apart, I headed toward the track where my train was now likely to be ready for boarding.

20

On my return from Oxford I felt shattered. Not only had I lost my way in my search for the table, but I was filled with the sense now that I had been betrayed by my dearest friend. Why had Roger not mentioned that he was seeing Antoinette? Or if he was not, why had he been to dinner with her and not told me? The Graceland incident festered within me as well, and when I had unpacked my broken suitcase, I seriously considered disposing of the visitor pamphlets I had taken from there, but ultimately, my habit of archiving got the best of me and I filed them away with my other items of memorabilia from the trip.

I had been contemplating whether or not to get in touch with Roger, and whether I should confront him on these matters, when one day, not long after I had returned, I happened to glance up and look out the window of the bookshop where I was looking at a magazine only to see Roger walking briskly by. It was before noon, a time when Roger rarely ventured so far abroad from his home. I hastily set down the magazine and rushed out the door. Perhaps I had intended initially to catch up with him and greet him. But he was walking fast, and I began to follow him. He seemed intent and strode with a sense of purpose. This also seemed unlike Roger, who tended to stroll and use his walks to gather inspiration for his writing, or to clear his head when he had been sitting too long.

I followed him for what seemed like quite a while, but may have only been ten or fifteen minutes, until he stopped in front of a brick row house, took out a small slip of paper and consulted it, perhaps checking the address. He then mounted the steps with confidence and rang the bell. The door opened, but I was unable to see who greeted him. He disappeared inside.

On that occasion, I contemplated waiting to see when he reemerged, but decided against it. Later, as these incidents became more habitual, I grew accustomed to waiting. Usually he remained at his destination for no more than an hour or two, and then he would reemerge, sauntering with a less purposeful gait, stopping to look at interesting sights along the route, as was his usual custom. At first I only followed Roger a few times a week. But soon it became a daily habit.

I am not proud; I am ashamed to write these lines now when I think of it. But at that time I felt that my actions were appropriate—justified, even. But the more I followed him, the less I felt I knew. After shadowing Roger for over a month, I was still unable to ascertain who or what his object was. These morning trips would occur no more than twice a week. I had taken to waiting near a shaded wall across from his house. I would stand near the wall beneath a tree each morning at about nine o'clock. Usually I might walk around the block a few times but returned to this spot regularly. I brought only a small notebook in which to jot down my impressions of the day and a packet of mixed nuts in case I needed quick nourishment. Sometimes I also brought along the pamphlets given to me by the man in the train station for reading material, as they were small and easy to fit in the pockets of my overcoat. Despite the logistical improbability that Roger was seeing Antoinette, and despite the fact that I had never spotted her anywhere on those days when he went out in the mornings, I was nonetheless convinced that it was she whom he sought.

A month and a half after I had begun following Roger, I was sitting at a rather dirty lunch counter in New York City eating a hotdog. I had asked the man behind the counter to bring me separately all the different fixings that were available for hotdogs. At first he was reluctant to accommodate my request, but I assured him that I would pay for the additional toppings. The counter faced out into the street, and between bites I stared anxiously through the frosty window. The frost had etched particularly delicate patterns on the windows that day, and I noted that though it was of the type that usually evaporates by midday, today the elaborate starbursts danced on windowpanes and sparkled even in the noontime sun.

I had not eaten a hotdog since my childhood experiments with taste. The long-forgotten texture of the processed meat, the piquancy of the relish, and the dulling effect of the ketchup returned me to that time in my childhood when I had worked so assiduously to catalogue every taste I could find. I took out my notebook, and trying to keep one hand clean, difficult with so many condiments, I created the kind of chart I used to make in my diaries, filling in the different unique sensations I derived from the processed meat.

It was a rude and dirty part of the city. I felt when I had entered the small restaurant that the other patrons were surprised to see an individual such as me enter their establishment. My own unease did nothing to convince them or me that my presence was perfectly natural. I leaned forward and gazed at the street again through the frosted window. Roger would be coming back soon. It had been an hour already. I had to remain vigilant.

That day, seated at the lunch counter, my attention was divided. Following Roger all the way to New York City had been a peculiar coincidence. Independent of my vigilance with respect to his movements, I had set out that day to take the train to New York in my pursuit of a different quarry: the table. After I had left Oxford, I had not expected to hear from Jim again, but one evening a few days previously, he had called me with the name of the dealer who had handled the sale. It had taken him some time, but he had managed to find the information somewhere among his papers. I immediately resolved to visit the dealer as soon possible, and thus, I had set out that morning to the train station to book my ticket to New York, choosing to forego my new daily habit of following Roger. As I looked out the window while the train was still in the station, to my great surprise, I had seen Roger hurrying along the platform. The train pulled out of the station moments later, and I had no way of knowing if he had boarded. For the next few hours of the journey, I had planned my approach. I could not walk through the train looking for him, as he would surely see me. What if he were to think I had followed him here? I would have to wait until we had arrived at our destination, make sure to be among the first passengers to disembark, and then find an observation post a short distance away.

This strategy proved successful. It emerged that he had boarded the train and was also heading for New York. I was able to spot him as he hurried through the station, unusually intent upon his object, as he always seemed to be these days. I was in a quandary, as I had secured an appointment with the antiques dealer one hour hence. But following Roger had become a part of my routine, and I found myself walking briskly down a series of Manhattan streets, always a little more than a block behind him. I reasoned that the dealer would be available all day. As it happened, he was not.

When I had finally seen Roger return to the train station in the afternoon, I set out to my original destination at the dealer's, only to find a note on the door: *I waited an hour but you did not come.* There was a phone number on the slip of paper, and when I called it later that evening, the dealer answered gruffly and agreed to meet me the next morning. After following Roger back to the train station just two hours after he had arrived in New York, I was forced to look for lodging for the night. After I had secured a room, I passed the rest of the day in the city's museums.

The meeting the following morning was short and yielded little. The dealer, a small man with bushy, brush-like hair clad all in black, was seated at an enormous desk wedged deep inside a dimly lit warren of antiques that seemed to protrude from every surface of the series of rooms. Rocking chairs hung from the ceilings; wardrobes towered over the narrow passageways like tall trees. It was not a showroom but a warehouse. To express his displeasure with my failure to appear on time the day before, the dealer kept me waiting as I sat in a chair by his desk, while he spoke on the phone at some length and shuffled through piles of invoices. When I was able to introduce my query to him, he thought for a few moments, looked through some files to refresh his memory (I had supplied the possible dates of the transaction), and then, squaring a pile of papers with his hands, he patted the pile and said, "Sorry, can't help you. I've found the record but this is confidential. All sales confidential." When I entreated him to make an exception, citing family research, he turned a deaf ear and waved me away. It was impossible to move him.

I walked along the street aimlessly, a feeling of desperation washing over me. This had been my last hope for finding the table. Seated on a park bench, my hands deep in my pockets, I watched the city dwellers bobbing to and fro as they engaged in various forms of exercise. Their hearts seemed light. They communed with their dogs and their children. If I still trusted Roger, I would have enlisted his aid in devising a way to break into the dealer's warehouse. He would have given me courage. But Roger had a secret that had corroded our friendship. He could neither be forgiven nor called upon. I was surrounded by enemies.

On the train ride home I decided I would have to get to the bottom of Roger's secret, whatever it took. But that way lay danger. I feared the consequences of confronting him. Roger was taller than me and I imagined he must be more agile. I would have to take great care to protect myself. Arriving home, I went to my desk and drew my grandmother's dagger, which I too was in the habit of using as a letter-opener from a drawer in my desk. From now on, I would keep this with me.

CORINTHIAN COLUMN
(detail)

21

One day, a week after my ill-fated trip to New York, I was standing outside of Roger's house. It was December and the air was crisp. I had been standing there for over an hour. It had been another sleepless night, during which I had listened to all my records of Brahms. I had decided to listen to my entire record collection in alphabetical order, to see if this would change my experience of the music. In those days, I was consuming a larger quantity of powder than usual, and I often paced about the room, stopping to take notes, rearranging my collections of *objets*, and eating very little.

As I took the well-travelled route between my flat and Roger's house, I availed myself of a packet of mixed nuts from a vendor. I stood slightly behind a tree eating the nuts one by one and contemplated the fact that the weather was unseasonably warm and that soon, with winter's chill, would be more difficult for me to undertake these vigils. I slipped my hand into the pocket of my coat and felt the cool handle of the dagger. Its presence comforted me; I knew I would be safe.

Suddenly, Roger emerged from his house. It was early for him to go out. He walked briskly and pulled his collar about his neck to ward off the cold. As usual, I kept about a block and a half behind him, stopping when he stopped, and ducking into doorways. It was soon clear that he was leading us to the train station.

Because of my suspicions that he was seeing Antoinette, I had been waiting for him to journey to Philadelphia. Until now, he had only gone so far as New York, where, I assumed, there must have been some assignation between the two of them. I was each day prepared for the eventuality of a trip to Philadelphia, and my pockets contained sufficient money to take the journey. No doubt he would need to furnish his wife with some kind of excuse to venture further. In the meantime, I had taken to imagining their correspondence. I imagined Antoinette writing him letters with a blue fountain pen on creamy white stationer's cards with her monogram across the top: "Let us meet somewhere between Philadelphia and Boston, my darling." Perhaps Roger would dash off more casual notes on bits of art paper, using a sketching pencil: "I will be there, my love."

Just as I suspected, after a visit to the ticket window, Roger headed toward the track from which a train to Philadelphia was set to depart in just twenty minutes. I quickly purchased a ticket for myself, and after surreptitiously ascertaining which car Roger had chosen, I boarded the train a few cars back. I was so excited after I sat down, I was unable to focus on my notes. It had been my practice since I had visited the antiques dealer to take notes each day about the table. I recorded in these notes my feelings about the lost object, and also strategies for tracking it down. I had, as I mentioned earlier, contemplated breaking into the warehouse and looking at the file on the sale, and even considered enlisting Roger's aid in this matter.

I felt, in a way, like a scientist, or better yet, like the anthropologist, who must refrain from intervening in the culture he observes, even if it is a matter of life or death. If he steps into the tableau he observes and questions the participants, how will he truly learn about their customs? Similarly, although I hoped that Roger was not seeing Antoinette, and would have dearly loved to stop him if he were, I felt strongly compelled to observe the truth and understand how these two members of different tribes had stepped out of their normal mating patterns to find some sort of attraction in one another.

Once in Philadelphia, Roger walked quickly out of the station and onto the street. Then he stopped abruptly and took out a map, rotating it slowly and looking at street signs. So he had not yet been to her house. I was relieved to find that my vigilance had paid off and I was witnessing his first visit. After gaining his bearings, he headed off down a large boulevard, and then down a series of side streets. It was already dark out and with the many trees along the sidewalks, it was easy enough for me to remain obscured from view. After a walk of some ten minutes, he reached a small brick apartment building, read the names on the buzzers, and pressed one. Moments later the door buzzed and he walked through.

I stood for a while looking up at the building. Now it was evening and it seemed unlikely that this would be a brief visit. Perhaps he would stay the night. What should I do? I needed proof of my suspicions. After about twenty minutes, I cautiously approached the building and walked up the stairs to the entryway. On the list of names was an A. GARNER. Next to her name was written #2b. I wondered if there was a way to get to the second floor; perhaps a fire escape? I stood uncertainly, glancing up at the second floor, where the lights were on but the shades were drawn.

Just then, a young woman, perhaps a college student, carrying two heavy bags of groceries, turned down the street. I wondered if I should go away so as not to look too suspicious lingering in the doorway, but worried that rushing away might look worse. I stood still and studied an advertisement for the delivery of pizzas that was hooked about the handle of the door. I looked up after a moment, wondering if she had walked by, only to find her coming up the steps where I stood.

"Can you get the door for me?" she asked. She seemed slightly out of breath.

"I'm sorry, I don't have a key," I replied nervously.

"Here," she said, handing one bag of groceries to me. She fished a key out of her pocket and pushed open the door, holding it open for me to follow. I was surprised by this development, but walked through the door holding her bag of groceries.

The door opened into a small foyer with mailboxes, after which the key was required yet again to get into the building itself. As we entered the second door I was unsure what to do with the groceries or where to go.

"I'm on the third floor," the young woman said, walking toward the stairs. It seemed I was to take her bag up for her. This presented me with an excellent cover, as I would be able to deliver the groceries to the third floor and then walk back to the second.

"Where are you going?" she asked suddenly as we climbed the stairs.

"To visit friends," I replied, hesitantly.

"Oh." She seemed out of breath. At the second floor landing, she turned and said, "Thanks for doing this. The grocery store is ten blocks away."

"Oh, yes, of course. Delighted." I was worried she would not keep going up the stairs, but she continued on her way. At the third floor, she opened another door that led down a long hallway carpeted in a dirty emerald green. The hall was dimly lit and painted in a chalky blue. She stopped in front of a door that was decorated with a small sign written in a language I had never seen before and put down the groceries. I stood nearby as she unlocked the door and walked in.

"You can put the bag on the kitchen counter," she called out to me.

I walked in the door, quite anxious by now, and looked

around. There was a small kitchen to the left, where I set the bag on the counter, next to the sink piled high with dirty dishes. Coming out of the kitchen, I saw that the rest of the apartment was all one room, with two doors off the side, one of which was open, and led to a bathroom.

The young woman began to unpack the bags noisily and put things away, seemingly unconcerned about my presence. I stood for a moment, uncertain as to what to do next.

"Very nice," I said, surveying the disarray of her apartment.

"Thanks." She began to empty a package of rice into a canister.

"Is the layout for all the apartments in this building the same?"

She turned slightly and looked at me curiously.

"No, no. The apartments on this side are all studios, but the ones on that side," she said pointing toward her refrigerator, "are all one bedrooms."

"Ah, I see." I didn't want to arouse suspicion by hurrying away, but on the other hand, I felt trapped in this small, untidy apartment.

"Well, you're all set, then?"

"Oh, yes, thanks!" she turned and smiled.

"I'll be going now," I said. Then I added, "to see my friends."

"Great! Thanks for helping me out!"

I bowed slightly to her and retreated through the open door, closing it as I left.

Now would be the moment of reckoning. I retraced my steps down the hall, through the hall door and down the stairs to the second floor. Here, too, there was a door to the hallway. I entered, and felt disconcerted by the change in color scheme. This hallway was carpeted in burgundy, a shade remarkably similar to the carpeting at the Russian Tearoom in Chicago. The walls were white. The lighting was much dimmer as some of the light bulbs appeared to be burnt out. I walked by apartment 2a, which would be the studio apartment similar to the one upstairs. The next door, marked 2b, was slightly ajar. I approached slowly, holding onto the handle of my dagger tightly for security. When I reached the doorway, I could see a sliver of light, and in that sliver of light, I saw Roger.

Roger was dressed in a rust-colored turtleneck and dark brown trousers. He was seated in an armchair, absentmindedly flipping through a large book of photographs. There was a drink on the table before him. I glanced at the wall above him to gain some insight into the occupant of this apartment. There was an old painting of a sledding scene hanging by a long wire from the white crown molding that edged the navy blue wall. Over the faint sound of the flipping pages, I heard the tread of an approaching step and the faint sound of jazz playing somewhere inside the apartment.

"Do you need anything to eat?" Antoinette's voice was clearly recognizable.

"No, no, I'm fine." Roger looked up and turned his face toward her, though I could not see her. I was startled by the look on his face, one of love, mingled with humility. Through the crack, I saw her hand reach down to put a coaster under his drink. This was when it happened. As I followed her hand, I focused for the first time on the table before him. I saw the outline of waxen fruits through a glass surface; I saw the mahogany casing. So it was Antoinette who had purchased my grandmother's table. She had been stunned, no doubt, as I had been, by its similarity to the one in Schiffley House. My pulse raced and my face felt hot.

22

I knew now what I had to do. All these weeks following Roger my mind had been unfocused. I had not understood fully what evidence I sought. But here, at last, I was confronted with irrefutable evidence of his treachery. I retreated slowly from the doorway, step by step, walking backwards so as not to take my eyes off the table, for the sight of it gave me a sense of purpose. When I could no longer see through the crack I turned and hurried down the hallway to the stairs. Once outside, I collected my thoughts. I would need to find a hotel, the sort of place that attracted persons of low reputation. That way my movements would not be regarded with suspicion. I would need also a hardware store, a liquor store and a druggist.

I felt a surge of confidence. I wondered if this was how it felt to be a great artist, who, wandering about on his quest for inspiration, suddenly turns a corner or looks across a room, and sees that building, or that person, which will provide him

with the subject matter he needs to be able to express his ge-
nius. The inspiration comes suddenly, the whole composition
of the masterwork, the colors needed, the size of canvas re-
quired; in a flash, all is known, when only moments before
confusion had reigned.

I walked quickly back toward the train station, where I
imagined I might find everything I needed. Sure enough, not
two blocks from the station, I saw a garish neon sign in blue
and white flashing the words "GALAXY HOTEL" from the
side of a narrow building. The A's on the sign were bright silver
stars. When I reached the entryway, I saw to my satisfaction
that the hotel encouraged hourly occupation as well as half-
day rentals. I entered the small dark office and enquired of the
gaunt older man at the desk about booking a room. I was able
to pay in cash and sign in under an assumed name. I took the
key and dropped it into the pocket of my greatcoat. As I turned
to leave, I asked, casually, if there was a drugstore in the vicin-
ity. There was, just a block away. Everything was falling into
place. Everything fit effortlessly into my plan.

At the drugstore, I asked the young lady at the counter to
recommend an effective sleeping draught. I had trouble get-
ting to sleep, I explained. I just needed an over-the-counter
remedy of some kind. The young lady was very pale, as were
her hair and lashes. She was blond, but in the glow of the store,
her hair appeared faintly green. She reacted slowly to my re-
quest. At first I wondered if she were hard of hearing, but then
I realized she was just thinking of a response.

"We have your naturals," she offered. "Your St. John's wort, your melatonin, what have you...." her voice trailed off.

"But are those effective?" I asked.

"I couldn't tell you," she responded flatly. "Then you've got your other options, they're right on the rack in front of you." She motioned vaguely toward a display that was not visible from her vantage point. "Your antihistamines and so forth."

"Are these good?" I asked. "Do they really make people fall asleep?"

"I imagine so."

Hurriedly, for I feared her soporific response might start to slow me down as well, I grabbed a handful of different boxes and paid for them.

"Can you tell me," I asked nervously, as she counted out the change, "can you tell me if there is a hardware store nearby?"

She looked up and gazed at me through her pale lashes and then continued to count. When she was done, she said, "Three blocks, turn left."

I thanked her and rushed from the store. Her instructions proved to be inaccurate, but only slightly so. It was four blocks, but with additional queries I made my way there. At the hardware store, I purchased a sturdy length of rope and a small saw, as well as some garbage bags. On my way back, I spotted a liquor store, an element of the plan I had forgotten about. The inventory was not impressive, but I did find a bottle of unremarkable sherry, which would have to do. Returning to the hotel, I climbed the creaking stairway to my room on the fifth floor. The hallway was full of odors, of smoke, of perfumes, of foods of all kinds. I entered my room and shut the door. It was quite small. Just enough space for a double bed and a small desk with chair. There was an attached bath, which pleased me, though initial inspection suggested it was not, or could not be, entirely clean. I sat down on the bed, which creaked, and emptied my pockets of the sleeping medicines. Then I set about preparing my plan so that all would be in order for Roger's arrival.

The next part would be more difficult. I would have to draw Roger to the room. By now it was quite late, and I felt reasonably certain that he would stay the night at Antoinette's. I took off my coat and laid it across the pillows, as I did not feel confident of their cleanliness, and did not want my head to touch them directly. Then I lay down on the lilac-patterned bedspread, which was made of some synthetic material. It was impossible to sleep, of course. I lay still for two and a half hours, listening to the sounds of human activity all around me. There was a romantic liaison occurring on the other side of the wall from the head of the bed. On the opposite side there were multiple voices of men talking and sometimes shouting. A card game, perhaps? Above me could be heard all manner of thumping and walking. I was uncertain what was taking place in that room, but I imagined a pogo stick, and perhaps an animal.

At 5 am, I rose, washed my face, and used the toilet. Then

I let myself out of the room, being careful to muss the covers sufficiently to make it look as though I had slept there during the night. Out on the street, I sought a dining establishment where I might partake of light refreshment to fortify me for the day ahead. I found a small diner that was open twenty-four hours a day. They served coffee and an assortment of breakfast foods round the clock. I ordered a cup of coffee, a poached egg and toast. The coffee was muddy—nearly undrinkable—but after emptying the contents of five small containers of cream into the cup and stirring in two packets of sugar, I was able to swallow it down. The egg was passable. There is not much that can be done to ruin a poached egg. But the butter for the toast was served in small plastic tubs and composed of a soy by-product. Alarmed, I pushed the bowl of these tubs to one side, and spread my toast instead with grape jelly.

Feeling refreshed, I stepped out into the street at around six o'clock and headed toward Antoinette's apartment. Once there, I positioned myself at a safe distance behind a tree, and waited. Roger did not emerge from the building until nine o'clock. He walked quickly. I surmised that he was hoping to catch the nine forty-five train. Once he had passed me, I waited until he was a block away and then trailed him. When we had got five blocks from the station, I cut to the left and jogged all the way to the entrance of the station. Then, smoothing my hair and catching my breath, I began to walk slowly away from the station. I saw Roger a block up, purchasing a newspaper from a metal box. I looked at the ground distractedly as I walked. When I knew I must be very close to him I looked up, suddenly, and started.

"Roger?" I called to him.

"Daniel!" Roger looked surprised to see me, and perhaps not a little irritated. "What are you doing here?"

"Research," I mumbled. "Schiffley House and all that," I added.

"Ah, yes." He looked at me closely. "Are you all right?"

"Yes, I..." I looked around. "Well, no, not really. It's been a difficult go with the archive."

"What's the matter?" he asked, surreptitiously eyeing his watch.

"Do you have time, Roger? I've not been well," I said, earnestly. "I need someone to talk to."

"I was going to catch the train," he said, "...but perhaps I could catch the next one, if it's urgent?"

"Please, yes," I said, trying to sound especially downcast. In truth, I felt quite excited. I could not believe how well my plan was working. It was exhilarating to see everything fall into place so neatly.

"Do you want to grab some coffee or something?" he asked.

"Actually, if you don't mind..." I hesitated.

"Yes?"

"If you don't mind, could we go to my hotel room?"

"Well okay, if it's close," he said hesitantly. His response was tepid, but it was good enough for me.

"I'm afraid it's terribly sordid," I added, "but I didn't bring much money with me and so I had to skimp on the room. I did get a reasonable sherry you might like," I added hopefully.

"Sherry? At this hour?"

I lowered my eyes, hoping to look crestfallen.

"Well, okay, then," he said, "we'll give it a try if it will cheer you."

I led him to the hotel, making small talk all the while. I noted that he did not attempt to explain his own presence in Philadelphia at all. Perhaps he thought I was distracted enough by my own sorrows, whatever they might be, that I would not think to ask or wonder. As I led him into the Galaxy Hotel, I noted his surprise at its seediness.

"It's very inexpensive," I explained to him on the stairs, as he ran his finger lightly over the stained and peeling wallpaper.

"I would imagine so."

A man stood outside the room next to mine, on the side where I imagined them to be playing a card game. He wore a black leather jacket, pin-striped trousers and a menacing scowl. I smiled at him.

"Good morning," I said.

He nodded slightly in response and looked Roger over carefully. I opened the door and ushered Roger in.

Roger looked around at the spare furnishings and the lilac bedspread.

"I wouldn't have expected to find you somewhere like this, Daniel," he said thoughtfully. "Is everything quite all right? Are you short of cash? Are you here for the dealers?"

"It isn't that," I said. "It's...it's depression. I've not been well. Research has been very, very trying. And there's the table," I added. "I just can't find it."

"Maybe you need a change of pace," he said, sitting down on the chair. "Maybe this project isn't good for you."

This had been the final test. To see if he would hide from me his knowledge of the whereabouts of the table. I was saddened, but not surprised, to see him fail it. The time had come.

"The sherry?" I asked.

"Sure, why not."

I took the bottle into the bathroom, where there were two glasses with white paper caps over them to suggest they had been sanitized. I looked out the door.

"I'll just use the toilet as well," I said, and shut the door behind me. Quickly I opened three packets of sleeping medicine and took two pills from each. They were capsules, and I emptied them all into one glass, and then filled both glasses with the sherry. Then I flushed the toilet, and stirred the medicated drink with the temple of my glasses. I washed my hands and reentered the room.

"Here you go," I said, handing him the glass. "I hope it is okay. I'm afraid I've no refreshments."

"That's okay," he said, taking a sip. "Blech," he added. "Really not good. What is this stuff?"

He looked up at me, and I did my best to look crestfallen again.

"Ah, but no matter. We'll rough it, won't we?" He patted the bedspread for me to sit down. "Tell me what's bothering you, Daniel. Let's get this sorted out."

I sat down and gingerly sipped the sherry. It really was not so bad as all that, but doubtless the medicines had ruined the taste. I made sure to scowl when I sipped it.

"I'm sorry this is so bad," I said. "I had hoped it would be decent, but the shop did not look promising."

"Ah well, better polish it off quickly," Roger responded, and, to my delight, he downed the remainder of the drink in one gulp.

"Yes, you are right," I said, feeling again that exhilaration of victory. I polished off my drink as well.

"So tell me about this research," he said, rubbing his eyes absentmindedly.

I began to make up some story about the Philadelphia Historical Society and their archives relating to Schiffley House. I spoke slowly and deliberately, hoping I would not have to speak for long. Sure enough, Roger started to yawn.

"I don't know why, but I'm feeling a bit sleepy," he said. He yawned again.

I pretended not to notice, but continued on with my tale. A clerk had brought me the wrong file, it concerned a different stately home; he would not admit his error. I had filed a complaint. Roger's eyelids were dropping shut. I spoke then to the supervisor and she had located the proper file, but it was missing a document.

He had now fallen asleep. I sat and watched him, not daring to move a muscle until I was sure he was fully asleep. Soon he began to snore lightly. I waited another ten full minutes, at which point, I expected that the medicine would well and truly spread throughout his body. Then I rose and fetched the length of rope, which I had hidden under the bed. Quietly, quickly, I wrapped it round and round Roger's body until he was com-pletely fastened to the chair. I finished it off with a square knot, which I was proud to remember from a few sailing lessons my mother had signed me up for when I was ten or eleven years old. Next the real work would begin. I went into the bathroom and poured myself another sherry, which I drank as quickly as the first. Then I set the glass down and gazed into the mirror. I wished I could immortalize this moment. The time had come. I returned to the bedroom and fished the dagger from my coat pocket.

23

I sat before Roger and contemplated his sleeping face. The muscles of his jaw were slack and his mouth open. His head had flopped to one side. The usual symmetry of his face was off. A pool of spittle was forming in a corner of his mouth. I imagined how Rodin must have felt when he began *The Thinker*. I reached out and picked up one of his hands. It was very warm. He twitched slightly and I started, but he was clearly asleep. I thought I would try for the wrist veins, as those are said to be the most effective for releasing blood.

I took my dagger and made a clean slicing motion across the veins of the wrist. But the cut was too superficial. I tried again. The impact was negligible. I was confused. I had been so sure of my plan. Clearly I would have to use more pressure. Perhaps the dagger was not so sharp as I had thought. I dragged the dagger very hard across the veins and a trickle of blood emerged. Then I tried it on the other side with the same effect. I was not convinced that these cuts alone would cause death. Perhaps I should try the jugular vein, though that would be harder to find and harder to cut into. Instead I continued to slice at the wrists, again and again. Now I was making some headway. There was enough blood that it had stained the cuffs of his shirt and my hands were turning pinkish. A splatter hit my glasses.

But suddenly, Roger's head jerked back. He roared, a terrible, deep and anguished sound, followed by a high-pitched shriek. His eyes were open, bloodshot. He was still firmly fastened to the chair, but he was able to stand, albeit slightly hunched over. He bellowed and bucked, twisting and turning. The chair knocked his glass from the desk with a crash. I sprang away in horror and crouched in the corner near the bed where I did not think he would be able to reach me.

"What have you done!" Roger yelled, the words slurred and laced with spittle. I didn't move, didn't speak. He looked down, and seeing his bloodied wrists, lunged toward the door, which he was somehow able to open by throwing the weight of his whole body sideways against it. I could hear doors opening along the hall as his shouts and screams traveled toward the stairwell. A series of crashing sounds heralding his successful descent down the stairs, and then I could hear nothing more. I should have stood up then, shut and locked the door and cleaned up the blood, but I was so startled by the turn of events that I didn't move a muscle.

A moment later, I heard someone enter the room, walking slowly and softly. The person was a woman. She peered around the corner and looked down at me. She was heavily made-up and wore a blond wig. She had on what appeared to be a school uniform of the type that young girls wear to Catholic schools, only the plaid skirt just barely covered her underwear.

"Hi there, honey," she said softly, reassuringly.

I smiled hesitantly. I had expected an officer of the law or perhaps a hotel staff member.

"How ya doing?" she asked.

"I'm fine," I said, though I'm not sure the response was convincing.

"I can see that," she said, glancing down at my dagger, which I still held in my fist.

"Why don't you give that to me, and I'll go get you a towel to clean yourself off with?"

She held out a hand, and I saw that she wore white kid gloves. I handed her the dagger, making sure not to extend the pointed end toward her.

"Thanks, sweetie. You wait right here. Don't move."

I did as she had commanded and waited.

A moment later, she returned, this time with a large sequined bag and another woman identically dressed.

"Now I want you to stand up," she said, gently, "and then lie down in the middle of the bed, with your arms out on each side."

I did as I had been instructed. The other woman reached into the bag and pulled out a handful of brightly colored nylon scarves with metallic dots that glittered slightly. She handed some to the first woman, and they each went to a corner at the head of the bed and took one of my hands and drew it to them. Uttering comforting words, they slowly and methodically tied my wrists to the posts of the bedstead with the scarves. I couldn't see what type of knot they made and wondered if such women knew nautical knots or some other technique.

During this process a couple of men had shuffled in. They wore undershirts and smoked cigars. Both held cards protectively in their hands. They gazed at me curiously.

"Is this the one that messed up the guy with the chair?" asked one.

"Yes," said the first woman. "I took his knife."

"Now they'll have your prints too!" chuckled the other man.

"I was wearing my gloves," she said.

"Always thinking," the first man grinned, and puffed on his cigarette without removing it from his mouth. The smell of the smoke on top of the heavy synthetic scent of the scarves was making me dizzy. I considered asking the men to extinguish their cigarettes but thought better of it.

"You call the police?" asked the first one.

"I told the front desk," said the second woman, nonchalantly. She sat down on the side of the bed and drew a pack of cigarettes from her bag. She took two from the package and lit them both with a pink lighter, then handed one to her friend. "They should be here soon," she added. The man nodded.

"What happened to the other guy, with the chair?"

"I expect there's an ambulance for him, but I don't think he was bad."

By this point, a third man with a handful of cards had entered. He was the one in the leather jacket I had seen in the hall when I had come up with Roger. He went into the bathroom and seemed quite happy to find the bottle of sherry. Showing it to the group, he asked if anyone wanted some.

"Shouldn't it be kept as evidence?" asked the second woman, blowing rings of smoke.

"He didn't die or nothing," argued the man. "We can just say it was empty when they come."

Everyone seemed to think that was a reasonable explanation, and one of the men went to get some more glasses. By the time the police officers arrived, the bottle had been emptied and the room was thick with smoke. I would have expected that the individuals assembled there would not be of the sort who would wish to be seen by the police, but such was not the case. Each one of them was greeted warmly by the two officers that entered, and the women were thanked for their work with the scarves.

"I can't undo your knots, you know that," joked the officer, motioning toward my wrists. The women undid the knots themselves and pulled me up into a seated position. The officer then fastened my wrists together with a pair of handcuffs.

"Weapon?" the other officer asked, looking around at the assembled group.

"Right here," the first woman handed him the dagger, which she had wrapped in a rainbow-striped scarf. The officer looked around and went into the bathroom. He picked up the boxes of sleeping pills and dropped them into a bag with the dagger.

"Anything else? That sherry was yours or in here?"

"In here," said one of the men.

"Empty?"

"Sure."

The officer guffawed and slapped him on the shoulder. They discussed the particulars of an upcoming card game while his partner looked around on the floor and picked up my coat, the rope, and the saw, which he found under the bed.

"Okay, let's take him in," he said, and pulling me to a standing position, they led me down the hall. Most of the doors were now open, and it seemed that the inhabitants of the rooms had been waiting for just this moment to peer out and get a good look at me.

Out in front of the Galaxy Hotel, an ambulance and two police cars, their lights flashing, were pulled up on the curb. The back of the ambulance was open, and some medics appeared to be tending to Roger.

"Will he live?" I asked.

"I'd imagine so," said the officer, laughing. "It takes a long time to kill someone with a letter opener."

"It was a dagger," I said.

"A what?" he asked.

"Nothing," I said, and ducked my head to climb into the back seat of the police car.

A third officer came and sat behind the wheel, and one of the other two came and sat next to me in the back. He turned and looked at me.

"One thing I can't figure out," he said to me conspiratori-ally.

"What's that?" I asked.

"What were you going to do with the saw?"

"That was to dispose of the body," I explained.

"Ah," he said, "Messy. Don't think you had enough paper towels to clean that up."

Both of the officers chuckled and slapped their knees.

"And the motive? What was the motive?" The officer at the wheel of the car turned to ask.

"He betrayed me."

"Love? Money?"

"No, no," I said, disgusted. "It was a matter of a table, and above all, bad taste."

Postscript

Thursday Lunch

12:07 pm

Succotash

(Components: Boiled carrot slices, approximately 1/3" thick, corn kernels, lima beans. Boiling lighter than on Tuesday, lima beans still closer to gray in hue than green. Thickness of carrot slices uniform, suggesting mechanized slicing, pre-packaging.)

<u>Texture:</u> Carrots soft, but not tender, corn moderately crisp, lima beans very soft.

<u>Taste:</u> *(component parts tested separately)* Carrots, slightly tart, as turnips, but mildly fragrant (nasturtiums?); corn, sweet, similar to caramel; lima beans, shoe leather, smell of damp leaves.

<u>Hue:</u> Carrots, yellowish-orange; corn, mustard-yellow; lima beans, gray-green (as noted above).

Added: Salt, pepper.

Antoinette says writing about one's crime can be therapeutic. She says it's something that should not just be done once, but over and over. For this purpose, she has given me a journal and told me to try to write in it every day. At first I certainly tried, but I did not find it the sort of writing that suited me. I found myself instead absentmindedly jotting down the particulars of my meals at the prison in just the same manner I had with the taste experiments of my youth. By and by, the journal began to be transformed into a record of my dining experiences, with less and less space devoted to the narrating of the incident that brought me here. Antoinette, as my writing teacher, does not approve.

Pork chop, broiled, fatty.
(Meat difficult to cut with plastic knives. Most diners opted for holding the chop with their fingers and eating from the bone, as with fried chicken.)
Texture: Rubbery.
Taste: Difficult to discern; mild. Wool/mushrooms (button type).
Hue: Light tan.
Smell: damp cotton.
Added: Salt, pepper (after initial findings).

Antoinette has given me a series of writing exercises that are meant to help me 'open up,' and 'express myself.' I am to try ten minutes of automatic writing a day, which she feels will help me access subconscious thoughts. I am also to write short descriptive paragraphs of things that interest me, except for food.

Mashed potatoes
(probably from flaked mix)
<u>Texture:</u> *Extremely smooth.*
<u>Taste:</u> *Margarine/milk; paper.*
<u>Hue:</u> *Ecru.*
Added: Salt, pepper.

Antoinette has promised that whenever I should return to the outside world, she will sell me the table. For now I content myself with sketching it. My roommate has been very kind in allowing me to decorate our walls with my drawings of the table. These sketches are executed partially from memory and partially with the aid of photographs supplied by Antoinette. I have completed approximately one hundred fifty of these, all told. I am sure that by the time my jailers see fit to release me from these four walls, I shall have created hundreds, possibly even thousands more.

Dessert: Bread pudding, strawberry ice cream.
Pudding
<u>Texture:</u> *Soggy.*
<u>Taste:</u> *Extremely sweet with strains of almond extract. Soaked in corn syrup most likely.*
<u>Hue:</u> *Unusually reddish; food coloring?*
Ice cream
<u>Texture:</u> *Melting, chunks of fruit.*
<u>Taste:</u> *Strawberry; likely a combination of artificially and natu-*

rally generated flavors; cream.
<u>*Hue:*</u> *Soft baby pink.*
Added: Chocolate sauce (paper taste here too/olfactory contamination?).

But it is the table to which my heart always returns. Gleaming, and smooth, its glassed-in fruits a symphony of lustrous color, the table is my one true source of inspiration. There is not an evening that goes by that I do not spend a moment visualizing its comforting silhouette before I sleep. Lying on my pallet in my cell, I close my eyes and picture first its outline, then the gently curved mahogany legs that reach up and embrace the ornate sides of the deep frame, and finally the glassy top beneath which nestle a cornucopia of perfectly crafted fruits. As I drift off to sleep I imagine myself curled up on its smooth surface, coasting peacefully through a cloudless sky.

Acknowledgments

I am indebted to many people for encouraging me to write fiction and for helping me shape *Taste* into its present form. A special debt of gratitude is owed to Brett Marty and Laurel Firestone, the earliest readers of the novel and my cheerleaders in writing fiction before I'd ever written a word. Thanks to early readers of the manuscript Chee Malabar, Manan Ahmed, Jessa Crispin, Amitava Kumar and Stephen Marlowe (who went on to become my esteemed and generous editor). It was Musharraf Ali Farooqi who kindly agreed to look at a draft and then introduce it by means of literary subterfuge to the wonderful Robert Wyatt, my mentor, step uncle and slave driver. With his help, *Taste* grew both in size and quality, and I also grew as a novelist, acquiring along the way a treasure trove of practical writing skills. I am also grateful to our wonderful designer, Jenn Manley Lee, for her help shaping the final product, and to Carl Sprague, Brett Marty, Kevin Sprague, Ruslan Sprague, Jason Dolmetsch, and many more for contributing their amazing talents to the making of the publicity trailer for *Taste*. Thanks also to Simona Mkrtschjan for a final once over with her keen copy editor's eye, and last minute proofreading and cheerleading from Prashansa Taneja and Eric Gurevitch. Finally, many thanks to my patient husband, Aaron York, for all his support, and Serafina, Ignatz and Otto, each for their own special contributions to this project.

ABOUT THE AUTHOR

Daisy Rockwell is a writer, painter and translator living in New England. Her previous publications include *The Little Book of Terror* and *Hats and Doctors*, translations of Upendranath Ashk's short stories. This is her first novel

CPSIA information can be obtained at www.ICGtesting.com
Printed in the USA
BVOW05s1227130414

350429BV00002B/5/P

M000191621

The Nathaniel Cook Book

THIS IS A W3K INTERNATIONAL PRODUCT

© 2019 Nathaniel Cook
Revised Edition (3rd)

All rights reserved. No part of this book may be reproduced or transmitted in any form or by any means, electronic or mechanical, including photocopying, recording, or by an information storage and retrieval system - except by a reviewer who may quote brief passages in a review to be printed in a magazine or newspaper - without permission in writing from the publisher.

Cover art contributions by author permitted under free media license terms and agreement with stock media at www.canva.com

ISBN 9780578809670

Published by Nathaniel E. Cook
Federal Way, WA

Printed in the United States of America

www.helpyourselfseehope.com

Dedicated to my beautiful family, we are now manifesting our destiny.

Δ

Family is the most important institution.

TABLE OF CONTENTS

-BREATHING SPACE-

*I*ntentions set motion towards impossible beginnings. Intentions are the will of human consciousness and human consciousness gives way to freedom.

And now is the moment

We've all been waiting for…

At peace, willing and able, awoke

Ready to even the score.

I'm gone.

You can call me the dead man walking,

My company uses the hush method,

That's no dead man talking

I'm on one

Yea my posture gets relaxed

When I'm feeling good

My status is verifiable in any hood.

I'm thankful for my goddesses and you should,

Fix your face if you ain't feeling this

Bad manners

Hey Black man,

Let me ask you a question?

Trash can

Hey black man?

What's the color of money?

I heard money was energy,

Now don't that sound funny?

Don't laugh…

Grab yo bag and hurry up and wait

I am here to stay,

Move over & be Great.

INTRODUCTION

You know why I don't care
about the opinions of others?
Because I love myself.
You know why I don't care about the judgment of
others? Because I'm thankful for everyone's help.

When's the last time this American nation
gave economic justice to a black man? They'll work
to convince you he's lazy, crazy or stupid before
allowing you to believe the reality of love.

Dr. King was assassinated knowing there
would be no social justice without economic justice.

When's the last time,
America gave economic justice to the black man?
Politics are the social distribution of economics, that
being said, when's the last time America cut a check
for the truth?

The following is an artistic self-expressed book of poetry, intended to encourage more Black Americans to read. I often have tried to be a provocative writer. Sometimes my content is cryptic and at other times not so much. All in all-the following was written to let you know someone out here loves you and wants you to be at peace.

You may not be at peace right at this very moment...
Be at peace with yourself
and at peace with your environment.
Be healthy and enjoy your freedom to be unique.

This is no stereotypical cookbook, but for artists, maybe it could be. Surprise - I am the one that wants you to be at peace. I can be a goofball. I enjoy writing books that sound like a dating profile. I enjoy making fun of people I'm "close to" and sometimes enjoy telling crude jokes to people at untimely moments. Eye have enjoyed being uncouth in the past because it helped remind me to laugh. Although it would seem as if some people are afraid to have safe,

honest fun when they refuse to laugh at crude jokes. It's possible that American psychology likes to breed psychopathic manners, disguised as political correctness. Oops--did I say that right after misspelling "eye"? Maybe I wrote "eye" to place a certain emphasis on self-reflection, rather than judgment.

When I write 'I', you may easily follow along, when I write ''eye', you possibly consider my art wrong. Hopefully, I don't lose you or seem crazy.

This book of poetry is filled with the ingredients of me. It's a little embarrassing releasing another edition of this book, but hey when you're working by yourself and you're not careful about small things, you can forget important details like page numbers. I have experienced first-hand why grace is so critical, in a land with fallible humans such as myself.

Nevertheless, here you are reading a book of poems. I wrote this introduction to yell stop! I wrote these words to push citizens across this nation to live better for themselves. I want virtuous people to join

hands in community, forcing corruption to be eradicated. I wrote these poems to give you a taste of my testimony.

WHISPERS OF A LEGACY

We're not here to be reckless

There's more to be done, press on towards glory

Pay no mind to the rear view,

Too often we get distracted

From those who are not in our shoes.

Walk Hard,

You have purpose.

The alternative is also present

Dual-ness in nature

Singleness in creation

Uniqueness by design

Completeness for the future,

USEFUL to all who care.

Even if it's only you

The angle of what is less, may be gone tomorrow

Consider the whisper of today.

BEHIND THE BARS

Vengeance is mine

Said the man who had awoken.

Let people treat you like shit for almost an omen

Played nice for way too long.

If you don't like me, then come kill me

Same old song

Reach out to me in conversation,

Tell me there is a problem.

That's the only thing required

What

Do we do to solve them

If you won't be honest about conflict,

Then you lose.

Fighters and lovers are both problem solvers…

So Choose

VIOLATION

Nobody wanted to shoot up a school…

More than I do
Nobody on this earth
Walks more serious than I do
My ego blames my childhood
My childhood blames the Army
The Army blames my childhood
Veterans Affairs ignore me
They come to your appointments
Go to a homeless shelter they say
I should stab you in the face
Make you look like helter-skelter.
And you're angry because of autism
And illiteracy
6 dead bodies try to haunt me
I thank the Lord, Knowing the devil wants me,
Jumping aboard
Demons stay in disguise
Shit jumping off board games

Steady aim, the trigger squeeze,

Women throwing pussy but fucking

Will make your stomach bleed

Look a man dead in his EYES

Tell him he's lying,

If he's not proclaiming the truth,

It means he's false flagging

In violation

SECOND

INTRODUCTION

Breathe.

It takes experience to find yourself,

It took failure for me to successfully accept the

present moment.

It takes getting out of your own way

It will take my death in order for me to live

Eternally.

Be at peace with yourself

and at peace with your environment.

Be healthy and enjoy your freedom to be unique.

There is a war going on outside, I'm sure you knew.
The war is psychological in nature, economic in
stature and social in function. What does that mean to
you?
Are you willing to suit up, and fight for what you
believe in?

Are you tired of laying down and playing nice to people that talk over you?

Are you not fed up with lies and deceit?

Are your bellies not hungry from the agonizing nights of famine?

Have you not been working and preparing to meet opportunities that lay before you?

Rise up celestial people and take what is yours,

All celestial beings get up and embrace your now! I dare anyone that claims to speak life, try and take my crown! I dare everyone that walks this earth to a challenge…I dare you to love yourself to the best of your ability and only then, do I dare you to judge another. Maybe you will find, it takes a lifetime to judge yourself.

I dare you to be gentle with yourself and mindful of your thoughts but transparent about them as well. I dare you to live your best life!

It's a difficult task, purifying the minds and hearts of a broken people. It has been the most difficult task doing it for myself. Yet, I am liberated by the

thoughts of men who came before me and I will live honestly rather than allow lies to eclipse my truth.

I challenge you to put 100% focus on yourself and only then, come and try to hate me for loving virtue. Stand fearless before anyone because love, especially expressed towards enemies requires passion.

THE ARRIVAL

Now that you've made it - Maintain

Help another reach the same

Not too many,

We agreed to one,

Remember-keep it simple

Don't try to do too much too soon

Trying to do too much with too little...

They are both the same.

Matter of fact just focus on yourself

And when you focus on yourself,

You'll remember, you never needed anyone else.

MY DADDY DON'T
LIKE ME

My Daddy said: I'm a better man than you

I looked over my shoulder

For who he was talking to

Confused by the echo,

No one else was in the room

Pointed to myself thinking,

Yea man -- time for me to leave.

He said: "I've climbed mountains

You'll never climb…

Been to valley's you'll never go thru…"

I thought I was supposed to be lifted

to the heavens by your spirit?

I had to open the Bible to some passage

To get my help,

I found it in 1 Kings surprisingly enough,

David said to his son:

"Be Strong & Show yourself a man…"

Are you ready to G up?

If not, go ahead and die bitter and afraid.

I hated the man I saw in the mirror

when I saw you

Your ego runs thru my veins

And so, I kill myself daily, to kill you.

I kill you every time I kill my ego.

I thank God for this feeling,

I thank God for freedom to be me.

Words can hurt, and provoke--and invoke

And choke--the living life out of a seed,

If you allow it.

I care if my words line up consistently,

Like verbs.

If they don't,

Then I have no reason speaking at all.

It's why the company's name is HUSH

Hush little baby,

My Daddy don't like me

And I really don't care

Because now I know

My daddy didn't like himself

THE ANGRY BLACK MAN DICHOTOMY

DICHOTOMY VS TRICHOTOMY

(The following was written as a philosophy paper, while I was studying at school. Although it may not provide a deeper context into 'who' I am, my hope is that it illustrates the intricacies of personhood that I have found on my journey to self-discovery.)

The angry black man: His name is Nate, a cocky student, two kids, psychologically, emotionally, and economically unstable. Mad at the world. Makes valiant attempts to do the right thing morally until time runs out, the point of death. Nate is a rebel, often referred to as the angry black man and too aggressive for his own good. His passion is threatening because it is extending beyond a point of moderation. Nate is like a bully that feeds on intimidation: His mind is a cauldron, filled with images and perceptions from anything offensively imaginable.

Since birth Nate has been perceived, in his native land, as public enemy number one. He is

a descendant of the subjugated person; he is arguably America's most subjugated person. Almost his entire existence, he was conditioned to be faithful to religion, hopeful, and deliberate about positive outlooks. Since his childhood, he has simultaneously been the victim of deceit and political manipulation--Like many others, he is used like a commodity, paraded about like any natural medium or means to an end. He is fed up with his current position at the bottom.

Nate struggles like a fish out of water with institutional lies and government, even at the municipal level. He is hungry for economic and social satisfaction. Organizations and individuals offer metaphysical or figurative solutions to his natural experience and this repulses him. Nate is rebellious in nature and now it is time to act. Regrettably, Nate has a victim mentality and is a victim of his own extreme nature. Caught in a vicious war within

himself, a vicious circle of misrepresentation and denial; Nate is angry.

The problem with anger is that it often fails to promote virtue. One cannot achieve virtue using anger as a rule of conduct nor can one promote anger to the ends within itself. For example, when maximum anger is expressed, a person becomes uncontrollable, lacking stability. Consider what it means to have stability within yourself or perfect equilibrium. Balance can be promoted within itself as a maxim or rule of conduct. It can be promoted in excess and will not falter or cause instability because balance only promotes excellence.

Nature is to be considered, when it comes to anger not meaning. Balance is evident in nature as it pertains to measurement for infinity. Both animals, limitless (in nature), and limited (in time to being extreme) equals polarizing. For example, the animals are similar to hot and cold temperatures; And both hot and cold

temperatures, in which we may reference anger is lukewarm when compared to the excellence of balance.

The docile black man: his name is Nathaniel. He is well-mannered, well-spoken, attempts to dress well to impress others, he is no stranger to shame. In contrast with his angry counterpart, Nathaniel holds a fear of image, and does nothing brash to tarnish it. He is often paranoid by the thought of failure. Nathaniel feels inadequate at times, doubts himself often and afraid to commit to almost anything due to fear. He's afraid to step out of the lines of political correctness, plain and simple, even when it comes to making money.

He is not to be pitied, he is also judgmental. In due time, his tepidness is recognized by others and he remains content for whatever scraps thrown his way.

Mediocrity is the anchor to his extreme nature; he lacks the will to fight, even when necessity calls-He is a threat to nothing.

Nathaniel has been a slave since birth; he was taught to always follow orders. He has been beaten for disobedience-used by society, as a means to produce a particular type of end and as a result he is the product for whatever environment he lives in. Nathaniel has been conditioned and his nature was brought about by a will that is not his own. He has grown to consider himself as less important than others. As a result of self-effacement, he has lost almost all reasonable ability to assert himself. Nathaniel the docile black man, is malleable and impressionable. He won't cause much trouble to any system or individual for that matter, especially those looking to use his talents or personhood.

Nathaniel has been a slave to fear for as long as he can remember, lacking confidence to

stand up for his own passions. He changes his genuine personhood to alleviate any discomfort for others or {even} the very thought of opposition.

Nathaniel is content with pessimism--He is a "coon"-the streets consider him a clown. Not to be trusted for lack of backbone but now the time has come for him to act.

Both characters: the angry Nate and docile Nathaniel are selfish. Both characters are slaves, taught and told how to behave, victimized and contained, generalized and categorized within a box. Ponder this perspective: that any person limited to a box will always be just that – a state of property. Both characters: Nate and Nathaniel are deficient, lacking virtue. Both characters are limited because both characters are extreme in nature. If you apply the philosophy of virtue ethics to both the docile personhood and overly aggressive person, you will see drastic change.

Nathan is the golden mean of the two extreme natures. Neither too aggressive nor docile, Nathan maintains almost a perfect poise (perfectum statera) where his balance is impeccable. He is virtuous in nature, mindful of focus, the importance of self-care and the necessary understanding when interacting with others. For example: the angry and docile men can both be smart & look handsome but do they possess moderation? Nathan is wise not clever. He is appropriate almost all the time; too wise to remain angry or docile. He is serious about self-governance, mindful of himself and others. Nathan possesses a tempered willingness to understand new experiences.

Balance is his only game, while genuine respect is his trademark. He is fallible to the extent that he is human and relatable but reliable only because of his direction. Grace and mercy are all about his life as he holds both hands open in which to receive and share from both. A blend

of 'athletics & academics' became his version of artistry. His opposition are emotions like jealousy and things that are unstable. Creativity is without limits in his imagination and his prophecies aim to promote harmony. According to this theory harmony is a necessary condition for balance. Virtue ethics overall can be a broad topic. Yet when anger is brought into the conversation, it seems to narrow the focus, and yet extend a trellis or framework of what we know to be a system for ethical behavior. If anger is to be perceived as an implicit emotion to be managed, rather than bad, then what is the aim of anger?

The aim of anger is of no concern because it exists only as any other emotion exists, within a person's character. Anger seems to exist as an emotional signal that some kind of action or speech is unpleasant. If anger is to be seen as virtuous, then a person's character should progress towards virtue and improve morally.

Anger in and of itself fails to improve a person's character overall. However, virtue ethics ideally help to make the expression of anger a model for others to use appropriately. For example, virtue ethics are more concerned with a person's character and less concerned with right acts. So when virtue ethics are applied, even a person who is experiencing anger may express their dissatisfaction in a way that is reasonable. It is critical to highlight that character building is a constant process for the way one thinks and feels. The ultimate hope may be to eliminate anger but while anger exists, use it against extreme forces which come to knock a person off balance. Improve your character with virtue ethics until you can stand with integrity in the midst of altering factors and organic environments.

MAMA DEAREST

If I could never tell you I love you again,

I would tell you I didn't want to be famous,

I wanted to be rich.

As a child I thought all famous people were rich.

I would tell you I didn't like that yellow sweater as

A young boy, but later in life

I wanted it more than any other piece of clothing.

Mama dearest,

I would tell you your heart is bigger than any woman

I've ever known.

This world doesn't deserve your strength.

I don't blame you for being afraid to rage either...

You are powerful beyond measure.

If I could never wrap my arms

Around your body again,

I would say that I gave this life all I had.

I would say art is an interesting intersect

Between hunger and taste,

While I assert the nature of a beast.

Different strokes for different folks,

But I kept swimming until my number was called.

If I could never say I love you again

I would say Cookie,

You the truth

And I'm thankful I stopped tolerating lies.

GET TO KNOW MY BEST ONE

I appreciate you and feel led to pursue

You can see the hunger in my eyes,

Romance ain't hopeless

I know you knew

Know the ace bandages

Get tossed for the jokers

A card scheme for the slow ducks,

With no gambit,

Wounded warrior projects but can't stand it.

I will always be a soldier,

Cold town,

The heart - ice colder,

Not speaking from pain, no hate, fear or shame,

Let go off all toxicity - no mind games.

Thank the Lord for my friend,

Promise we'll ride to the end,

Got my loyalty back,

Fearless through thick and thin.

Viciousness begins with conclusions

Lungs filled with breath in the air,

Call me gone with the wind.

I want to be a poet

No more waiting for some prophet

To start cussing, time to show it

Here's a literacy level for you:

She been had the juice

I can take any stereotype and fill it ripe

Pluck the fruit

Then ask any Queen, who got the coochy juice?

Don't rub it

Let it run down

Gangstas don't run from the town,

We run towards glory

Get to know me, get to know my story.

FAMILY GIFT

Break the generational curse

Good luck first born

Do the generational work

Go head – it's your turn

You want to feed your family?

You best feed yourself

Cause when that moment comes,

They gone ask for your help

Drowning in divorce – no reconciliation,

Swallow hard and put a hand up

Go ahead and be the black sheep,

Maybe another brave soul will put a hand up

Relax…take a breather.

There's 100 ways to skin a religious cat,

Perceive past all conditioning now,

Indoctrinate that.

To all my princesses,

Thinking sex is a weapon,

Some people use money

For adequate deception.

Renew your mind, ignore hate

Transform your life, make mistakes

And be honest with yourself,

Know that life is great.

This just some food for thought,

Clean your plate.

Give a shout-out to single dads

Kissing they kids thru pictures

And to the single mom's,

I call you bitter one's witches

Nah that's the spirit of legion

To whom-I used to pray my allegiance

Praying for peace rather than vengeance

Understanding to all wife beaters and man eaters.

Reconciliation is the plan,

Call it family construction.

I repeat, Reconciliation is the plan.

Build!

FAMILY CURSE

The family curse lies in brokenness

Get it?

The family lies and there is brokenness

Liars, Broke and Bougie

Now what kinda combination is that?

The family was either cursing or spelling,

But either way, they're just words.

Lies, as in you sense something's off…

Ask what's wrong, but get "nothing, I'm fine!"

Lies are like fine lines

Can your family cross anytime?

No passive aggressive behavior,

Learned from the other side.

Judging eyes blind the third eye

Relatively struggling to see clearly

It used to be, brokenness was handed down

Like a beautiful family heir loom.

Generational poverty because God forbid you actually

Have enough money to thrive upon.

They can keep the Polaner all-fruit

Would you please pass the gray coupon?

It reads "survival special three for 1"

Disrespect me and I'll get a gun

If the spirit of fear is put in the middle son,

Then justify why it shouldn't be passed

To the next generation

Let us pass ego, trauma, and financial illiteracy over

Stress relieving ideas, ownership,

And the importance of celebrating uniqueness.

Since before 1985 sweetness

You will follow suit,

Or grab a suitcase and get your own new clothes

That's your choice

Either stay and be cursed

Or take this heart-felt prayer with you

As you work to break it.

The family curse of lies and brokenness.

MICROPHONE CHECK

All black check, Crisp cut check

Nike check, Denim vest check

Burgundy check

Swerving me check

I'll buy another without writing a check

Fresh to death, fashion check

Ambiance in my fiancée check

Nosy press,

Four play check

Dangerous baby made check

Sex game check

No hate check

Negative energy gets an x check

53 grand to my ex check

Still preaching facts perfect context

Renaissance yes, Brand names less

Important but it's all over a game check

Just know it's written I did it to blame a check

And you do it late chasing the same CHECK.

A PAGE FROM MY RHYME BOOK

To perceive death as an event,

That's all it is?

Scholars get to doing expositions in shit

Death is simple without the sting

Relax while a woman sings

This how I know you not for me

You make me want to treat you like

You owned by the streets

Brush your teeth

Wash my tongue with your gun

Is my essence your juice?

There's nothing toxic about healthy roots

Don't let your left know what your right is doing

Whoever said that is…

In a vicious circle

And struggle thru it.

Some use every accomplishment

Painful to avoid good medicine,

One sight of pain, pop a sedative,

Natural selection.

We don't cope we have shalom,

Gentiles alike peace!

Make your intentions explicit,

Be genuinely kind to speech.

Be serious about your dreams

Love on yourself and be cupid…

~~Don't be stubborn stupid~~

Learn how to grab a bag

More than anything show more respect

Learn to master a craft.

THE HOURGLASS

I woke up one day and the world was different.

Everything around me,

Before I went to sleep was in disarray

Almost in complete chaos.

The men were arguing with men

The women were arguing with women

The children were scattered,

No one seemed to understand anyone.

Things had changed

When I awoke the next morning

Everyone was still present, and in their own skin

But their actions were different.

Attitudes shifted,

People were now on their best behavior

Social interaction was blanketed,

With a false calm during the night.

Caricatures now awake.

Order was in the midst.

Along with insincerity and fearful lies

Lives asleep

Though eyes on a sandy beach

In the hour glass.

PEACEFUL

BLACK MAN

Let me ask you a question, angry black man?

What do you want?

Do you want to feel better?

Stop everything you're doing

And focus on yourself,

Are you breathing?

More importantly, did you need anyone's help?

Realize you got the stuff,

Dreams are made of,

Magic is in the air, and you just breathed it in.

Inhale some more opportunity

Through your nostrils.

Only you can get in your way

Church folk call that sin

To win, requires

Self-discipline

You are in control of your thoughts, only you

Pick up your feet and prove

Bitter hate is wrong.

Make your next move your best move,

You are free to choose

You alone, have one soul to save,

It's your own.

You cannot take anyone with you

On this journey of experience,

The entire globe is your home.

Did you not realize you were safe here?

Is that why you were angry?

Be mindful sure,

But relax while you focus

On that magical breath.

BORN TO DIE

Rushing a project is none

Rushing a lap minus one

Rushing like Russians couple two

Brushing. To clean what I do

Victory laps minus Nipsey is white people

Screeching for breakfast is

Work when I eat

Play

Clean

Work everyday

Rest

Pray

Follow Me

Say

I pray I die today

THE 13TH TRIBE

This for the soldiers,

Steady building like gentrification.

Love hard

To destroy institutions that protect discrimination

Philosophy of language

The teacher of social implications.

Cultural differences are not justification for war,

Yet violence is necessary until all of Heaven

Is restored

Allow this for consideration,

Push against assimilation,

Yet get segregation,

Simplify the degradation

Boil it down to separation or distinction,

Independence is practicing a declaration

Of repentance.

Prepare an offer of reparations

No time to threaten your agitations

and manipulations.

Shout-out to the young Gods and Goddesses,

Queens and Kings let freedom ring.

All throughout the tribes of Judah, Benjamin, Simeon,

Levi, Issachar, Zebulun, Reuben, Joseph, Dan,

Naphtali, Gad, Asher

O' but if you didn't hear your name called

Better do your research,

Get to studying

Cuz when knowledge gets to dumping A's

30 round clips may persuade you to book it

Say "Know Justice - Know Peace"

With another lower case K

Who's willing to stay the course?

Take viciousness by the throat?

Who's willing to kill

For honesty, transparency and compassion?

12 tribes were called,

While more than one drank what they thought was
kool-aid

But choked, on shed blood

Stay focused – Is it possible--we are not the same!

TO MY BROTHERS

I am not perfect but it's a good thing. I am what I am

We are choices and intentions

We are energy and while being complex we simply

possess ourselves.

Don't let commercial clones steal, kill or destroy

Your originality

I know this is random,

I try not to do anything out of anger,

It puts static in the flow.

Always prefer to keep it smooth.

Just know

That at one point, I was limited by fear

Similar to time - fear is of no concern.

Be wiser

Be greater than I,

By producing greater works

Have fun doing it.

Be patient because every season changes,

As the Most High commands.

Extend grace to our neighbors

Judge only yourself

And do not misrepresent how you feel.

Experience is a blessing.

And blessings extend beyond just one temple.

Love!

TRUTH SERUM

Look I'm not talking about fictitious Jesus

When I say The Christ

I'm talking about Yoshua of the Bible.

With real passion…The real Christ,

Who's skin was blacker than my Grandfather's

Who's hair was as strong as my first born son.

Truth serum is about the inspiration

The holy spirit may duel with a thing

but the holy spirit sanctifies anything it touches

The Christ was righteous

The passion of the Christ was pure

Mine

Not even close

I have been distracted by beautiful women,

With seducing lips

And curvy hips

Distractions can be wavy baby

Lacking focus can make you crazy.

We call it drifting

No sifting

My passion

To plan another course of action

Because heaven prevails

PROCEED TO HAPPINESS

If heaven is a mindset,

Then heaven is a choice.

The same way thoughts precede the voice

Be transparent about your heart

You only have one

One heart

One mind

One mouth

One life,

With the potential to harmonize,

With others that also choose this side.

Choose grace for mistakes,

Among other things eternally

Choose faith,

To jump beyond death to eternity.

The gates of hell

Surprisingly border heaven,

Kinda like the number 6 borders 7.

We are blessed!

There is no luck when you repent,

From your past.

Love your enemies…because

If there will always be wars and rumors of wars,

Peace enjoys the last laugh.

Peace amidst sirens ringing

Peace in the midst of death and dying.

No convincing story telling you to join us,

You may stay right where you are

But enjoy it while it lasts.

The process

Of being Happy

~~Is the result of accepting the truth~~

~~By hearing the voice.~~

Self-Love is the key to eternal life

Contributions by

Chris Fuller
Joseph Gibson
"Sumo" Ventura Elisaia Aiomata Jr.
Matthew Cloutier
Tamika Hogan
Ariana Davis
Michael Yang
Brian Murray
Elliot Flett
Jonathan Cook
Ethan Cook
Dr. Dwight Cook
&
Andrew Powers

Acknowledgments

Thank you to my Lord and savior:

Love Most High

Made in the USA
Middletown, DE
30 March 2022

63380598R00033